TRUTH IS GOD

[Gleaning from the writings of Mahatma Gandhi
bearing on God, God-Realization and the Godly Way]

By
M. K. GANDHI

Compiled by
R. K. PRABHU

NAVAJIVAN PUBLISHING HOUSE
AHMEDABAD - 380 014

Rupees Forty

© Navajivan Trust, 1955

First Edition, 3,000 Copies, May 1955
Twentyfirst Reprint, 3,000 Copies, September 2013
Total : 56,000 Copies

ISBN 978-81-7229-003-0

Printed and Published by
Vivek Jitendra Desai
Navajivan Publishing House
Ahmedabad-380 014
INDIA

Phone : 079 - 27540635, 27542634
E-mail : jitnavjivan10@gmail.com
Website : www.navajivantrust.org

FOREWORD

The Navajivan Managing Trustee has fallen a victim to the prevailing fashion and illusion. He wants a 'Foreword' from me to a book of selections from Gandhiji's writings dealing with religion and God. The subject as well as the author ought to have saved Shri Jivanji from this foreword-hunger. But so strong is fashion that in spite of everything he has done like others and wants me to do what is wholly unnecessary.

God and therefore religion are fundamental necessities for normal healthy life – to the individual as well as to nations. Here in this book the reader will find Gandhiji speaking from his heart on various occasions in the course of thirty years of the maturest period of his life. What a modern man who did very great things thought on the subject of God and religion cannot fail to be instructive to educated men and women in these difficult days.

"We the human family are not all philosophers. Somehow or other we want something which we can touch, something which we can see, something before which we can kneel down. It does not matter whether it is a book or an empty stone-building or a stone-building inhabited by numerous figures": so wrote Gandhiji, defending temple-worship on the background of other prevailing religions.

"Hindu Dharma is like a boundless ocean teeming with priceless gems. The deeper you dive, the more treasures you find," said Gandhiji.

Any one who desires to understand what sort of a man the Father of the Nation was, must read this book.One may not want to learn anything about religion that is not in our Shastras or in other religious books. But here is a facet of the mind of a great man we love and to whom the nation is grateful. It has a value over and above a book of religious instruction.

Madras, 11-4-'55   G. Rajagopalachari

CONTENTS

Chapter

FOREWORD iii

1 MY QUEST 1

2 GOD IS 4

3 GOD ALONE IS 7

4 TRUTH IS GOD 11

5 GOD IS LOVE 15

6 GOD IS TRUTH – KNOWLEDGE – BLISS 18

7 GOD AND NATURE 20

8 GOD AS DARIDRANARAYAN 24

9 THE VOICE OF GOD 26

10 GOD-REALIZATION 30

11 THE PATH OF AHIMSA 34

12 PRAYER – THE ESSENCE OF RELIGION 39

13 WHY PRAY? 42

14 HOW, TO WHOM AND WHEN TO PRAY 46

15 FASTS 49

16 THE ETERNAL DUEL 53

17 SELF-PURIFICATION 55

18 VALUE OF SILENCE 57

19 EQUALITY OF RELIGIONS 59

20 TOLERANCE 63

21 CONVERSION 65

22	WHY I AM A HINDU	73
23	BUDDHISM, CHRISTIANITY AND ISLAM	76
24	GOD AND GODS	79
25	TEMPLES AND IDOLS	84
26	TREE-WORSHIP	88
27	REASON AND FAITH	90
28	SCRIPTURES	92
29	THE MESSAGE OF THE GITA	95
30	BEAUTY IN TRUTH	104
31	RAMANAMA	108
32	NATURE CURE	111
33	UNITY OF ALL LIFE	115
34	WHAT IS BRAHMACHARYA	119
35	STEPS TO BRAHMACHARYA	123
36	MARRIAGE, A SACRAMENT	127
37	GOSPEL OF NON-POSSESSION	130
38	WORK AS WORSHIP	133
39	SARVODAYA	137
40	ETHICS OF THE ATOM BOMB	140
41	PEACE ON EARTH	142
42	OBITER DICTA	145
	NON-ENGLISH WORDS WITH THEIR MEANINGS	155
	SOURCES	161
	INDEX	162

TRUTH IS GOD

TO THE READER

I would like to say to the diligent reader of my writings and to others who are interested in them that I am not at all concerned with appearing to be consistent. In my search after Truth I have discarded many ideas and learnt many new things. Old as I am in age, I have no feeling that I have ceased to grow inwardly or that my growth will stop at the dissolution of the flesh. What I am concerned with is my readiness to obey the call of Truth, my God, from moment to moment, and therefore, when anybody finds any inconsistency between any two writings of mine, if he has still faith in my sanity, he would do well to choose the later of the two on the same subject.

Harijan. 29-4-M1 p.2   M. K. GANDHI

1. MY QUEST

I am but a seeker after Truth. I claim to have found a way to it. I claim to be making a ceaseless effort to find it. But I admit that I have not yet found it. To find Truth completely is to realize oneself and one's destiny, i.e. to become perfect. I am painfully conscious of my imperfections, and therein lies all the strength I possess, because it is a rare thing for a man to know his own limitations.

Young India, 17-11-'21

If I was a perfect man, I own I should not feel the miseries of neighbours as I do. As a perfect man I should take note of them, prescribe a remedy, and compel adoption by the force of unchallengeable Truth in me. But as yet I only see as through a glass darkly and therefore have to carry conviction by slow and laborious processes, and then, too, not always with success. That being so, I would be less than human if, with all my knowledge of avoidable misery pervading the land and of the sight of mere skeletons under the very shadow of the lord of the Universe, I did not feel with and for all the suffering but dumb millions of India.

Young India, 17-11-'21

I am but a poor struggling soul yearning to be wholly good-wholly truthful and wholly non-violent in thought, word and deed, but ever failing to reach the ideal which I know to be true. It is a

1

painful climb, but the pain of it is a positive pleasure to me. Each step upward makes me feel stronger and fit for the next.

Young India, 9-4-'25

I know the path. It is strait and narrow. It is like the edge of a sword. I rejoice to walk on it. I weep when I slip. God's word is : 'He who strives never perishes.' I have implicit faith in that promise. Though, therefore, from my weakness I fail a thousand times, I will not lose faith but hope that I shall see the light when the flesh has been brought under perfect subjection as some day it must.

Young India, 17-6-'26

I have not seen Him, neither have I known Him. I have made the world's faith in God my own and as my faith is ineffaceable, I regard that faith as amounting to experience. However, as it may be said that to describe faith as experience is to tamper with truth, it may perhaps be more correct to say that I have no word for characterizing my belief in God.

Autobiography, 1948, p. 341

I claim to be a votary of truth from my childhood. It was the most natural thing to me. My prayerful search gave me the revealing maxim *Truth is God,* instead of the usual one *God is Truth.* That maxim enables me to see God face to face as it were. I feel Him pervade every fibre of my being.

Harijan, 9-8-'42

Ahimsa is my God, and Truth is my God. When I look for Ahimsa, Truth says, 'Find it through me.' When I look for Truth, Ahimsa says, 'Find it out through me.'

Young India, 4-6-'25

To see the universal and all-pervading spirit of Truth face to face one must be able to love the meanest of creation as oneself. And a man who aspires after that cannot afford to keep out of any field of life. That is why my devotion of Truth has drawn me into the field of politics; and I can say without the slightest hesitation, and yet in all humility, that those who say that religion has nothing to do with politics do not know what religion means.

Autobiography, 1948, p. 615

I am endeavouring to see God through service of humanity, for I know that God is neither in heaven, nor down below, but in every one.

Autobiography, 1948, p. 615

I have no desire for the perishable kingdom of earth. I am striving for the Kingdom of Heaven which is Moksha. To attain my end it is not necessary for me to seek the shelter of a cave. I carry one about me, if I would but know it. A cave-dweller can build castles in the air whereas a dweller in a palace like Janak has no castles to build. The cave-dweller who hovers round the world on the wings of thought has no peace. A Janak though living in the midst of 'pomp and circumstance', may have peace that passeth understanding. For me the road to salvation lies through incessant toil in the service of my country and therethrough of humanity. I want to identify myself with everything that lives.

Young India, 3-4-'24

I want to realize brotherhood or identity not merely with the beings called human, but I want to realize identity with all life, even with such things

as crawl upon earth. I want, if I don't give you a
shock, to realize identity with even the crawling
things upon earth, because we claim descent from
the same God, and that being so, all life in
whatever form it appears must be essentially one.
    Young India, 4-4-'29

There is no such thing as 'Gandhism', and I do
not want to leave any sect after me. I do not claim
to have originated any new principle of doctrine. I
have simply tried in my own way to apply the
eternal truths to our daily life and problems. Truth
and non-violence are as old as the hills. All I have
done is to try experiments in both on as vast a
scale as I could do. In doing so I have sometimes
erred and learnt by my errors. life and its problems
have thus become to me so many experiments in
the practice of truth and non-violence.
    Harijan, 28-3-'36

My faith in truth and non-violence is ever-
growing, and as I am ever trying to follow them in
my life, I too am growing every moment. I see new
implications about them. I see them in a newer
light every day and read in them a newer meaning.
    Harijan, 2-3-'40

2. GOD IS

There is an indefinable mysterious Power that
pervades everything. I feel it, though I do not see
it. It is this unseen Power which makes itself felt
and yet defies all proof, because it is so unlike all
that I perceive through my senses. It transcends
the senses.

But it is possible to reason out the existence of

God to a limited extent. Even in ordinary affairs we know that people do not know who rules or why, and how he rules. And yet they know that there is a power that certainly rules. In my tour last year in Mysore I met many poor villagers and I found upon inquiry that they did not know who ruled Mysore. They simply said some god ruled it. If the knowledge of these poor people was so limited about their ruler I, who am infinitely lesser than God, than they than their ruler, need not be surprised if I do not realize the presence of God, the King of kings. Nevertheless I do feel as the poor villagers felt about Mysore that there is orderliness in the universe, there is an unalterable law governing everything and every being that exists or lives. It is not a blind law; for no blind law can govern the conduct of living beings, and thanks to the marvellous researches of Sir. J. C. Bose, it can now be proved that even matter is life. That law then which governs all life is God. law and the lawgiver are one. I may not deny the law or the lawgiver, because I know so little about It or Him. Even as my denial or ignorance of the existence of an earthly power will avail me nothing, so will not my denial of God and His law liberate me from its operation; whereas humble and mute acceptance of divine authority makes life's journey easier even as the acceptance of earthly rule makes life under it easier.

I do dimly perceive that whilst everything around me is ever changing, ever dying, there is underlying all that change a living power that is changeless, that holds all together, that creates, dissolves and recreates. That informing power or spirit is God. And since nothing else I see merely through the senses can or will persist, He alone is.

And is this power benevolent or malevolent? I see it is purely benevolent. For I can see that in the midst of death life persists, in the midst of untruth truth persists, in the midst of darkness light persists. Hence I gather that God is Life, Truth, Light. He is Love. He is the Supreme Good.

But He is no God who merely satisfies the intellect, if He ever does. God to be God must rule the heart and transform it. He must express Himself in every smallest act of His votary. This can only be done through a definite realization more real than the five senses can ever produce. Sense perceptions can be, often are, false and deceptive, however real they may appear to us. Where there is realization outside the senses it is infallible. It is proved not by extraneous evidence but in the transformed conduct and character of those who have felt the real presence of God within.

Such testimony is to be found in the experiences of an unbroken line of prophets and sages in all countries and climes. To reject this evidence is to deny oneself.

This realization is preceded by an immovable faith. He who would in his own person test the fact of God's presence can do so by a living faith. And since faith itself cannot be proved by extraneous evidence, the safest course is to believe in the moral government of the world and therefore in the supremacy of the moral law, the law of Truth and Love. Exercise of faith will be the safest where there is a clear determination summarily to reject all that is contrary to Truth and Love.

I cannot account for the existence of evil by any

rational method. To want to do so is to be coequal with God. I am therefore humble enough to recognize evil as such. And I call God long suffering and patient precisely because He permits evil in the world. I know that He has no evil. He is the author of it and yet untouched by it.

I know too that I shall never know God if I do not wrestle with and against evil even at the cost of life itself. I am fortified in the belief by my own humble and limited experience. The purer I try to become, the nearer I feel to be to God. How much more should I be, when my faith is not a mere apology as it is today but has become as immovable as the Himalayas and as white and bright as the snows on their peaks? Meanwhile I invite the correspondent to pray with Newman who sang from experience :

lead, kindly light, amid the encircling gloom,
    lead Thou me on :
The night is dark and I am far from home,
    lead Thou me on.
Keep Thou my feet, I do not ask to see
The distant scene; one step enough for me.
    Young India, 11-10-'28

3. GOD ALONE IS

To me God is Truth and Love; God is ethics and morality; God is fearlessness. God is the source of light and life and yet He is above and beyond all these. God is conscience. He is even the atheism of the atheist. For in His boundless love God permits the atheist to live. He is the searcher of hearts. He transcends speech and reason. He knows us and our hearts better than we do ourselves. He does not take us at our word for He knows that we often do not mean it, some knowingly and others unknowingly. He is a personal God to those who need His personal presence. He is embodied to those who need His touch. He is the purest essence. He simply Is to those who have faith. He is all things to all men. He is in us and yet above and beyond us. One may banish the word 'God' from the Congress but one has no power to banish the thing itself. What is a solemn affirmation, if it is not the same thing as in the name of God? And surely conscience is but a poor and laborious paraphrase of the simple combination of three letters called God. He cannot cease to be because hideous immoralities or inhuman brutalities are committed in His name. He is long suffering. He is patient but He is also terrible. He is the most exacting personage in the world and the world to come. He metes out the same measure to us as we mete out to our neighbours-men and brutes. With Him ignorance is no excuse. And withal He is ever forgiving for He always gives us the chance to repent. He is the greatest democrat the world knows, for He leaves us 'unfettered' to make our own choice between evil and good. He is the greatest tyrant ever known, for He often dashes the cup from our lips and under cover of free will leaves us a margin so wholly inadequate as to provide only mirth for Himself at our expense. Therefore it is that Hinduism calls it all His sport — lila, or calls it all an illusion — Maya. We are *not*. He alone Is. And if we will be, we must eternally sing His praise and do His will. let us dance to the tune of His Bansi — flute, and all would be well.

Young India, 5-3-'25

Advaitism and God

[In answer to a friend's questions, Gandhiji wrote:]

I am Advaitist and yet I can support Dvaitism
(dualism). The world is changing every moment,
and is therefore unreal, it has no permanent
existence. But though it is constantly changing, it
has a something about it which persists and it is
therefore to that extent real. I have therefore no
objection to calling it real and unreal, and thus
being called an Anekantavadi or a Syadvadi. But
my Syadvada is not the Syadvada of the learned, it
is peculiarly my own. I cannot engage in a debate
with them. It has been my experience that I am
always true from my point of view, and am often
wrong from the point of view of my honest critics.
I know that we are both right from our respective
points of view. And this knowledge saves me from
attributing motives to my opponents or critics. The
seven blind men who gave seven different
descriptions of the elephant were all right from
their respective points of view, and wrong from the
point of view of one another, and right and wrong
from the point of view of the man who knew the
elephant. I very much like this doctrine of the
manyness of reality. It is this doctrine that has
taught me to judge a Mussalman from his own
standpoint and a Christian from his. Formerly I
used to resent the ignorance of my opponents.
Today I can love them because I am gifted with the
eye to see myself as others see me and vice versa.
I want to take the whole world in the embrace of
my love. My Anekantavada is the result of the twin
doctrine of Satyagraha and Ahimsa.

I talk of God exactly as I believe Him to be. I

believe Him to be creative as well as non-creative.
This too is the result of my acceptance to the
doctrine of the manyness of realty. From the
platform of the Jains I prove the non-creative
aspect of God, and from that of Ramanuja the
creative aspect. As a matter of fact we are all
thinking of the Unthinkable, describing the
Indescribable, seeking to know the Unknown, and
that is why our speech falters, is inadequate and
even often contradictory. That is why the Vedas
describe Brahman as 'not this', 'not this'. But if He
or It is not this, He or It is. If we exist, if our
parents and their parents have existed, then it is
proper to believe in the Parent of the whole
creation. If He is not, we are nowhere. And that is
why all of us with one voice call one God
differently as Paramatma, Ishwara, Shiva, Vishnu,
Rama, Allah, Khuda, Dada Hormuzda, Jehova,
God, and an infinite variety of names. He is one
and yet many; He is smaller than an atom, and
bigger than the Himalayas. He is contained even in
a drop of the ocean, and yet not even the seven
seas can compass Him. Reason is powerless to
know Him. He is beyond the reach or grasp of
reason. But I need not labour the point. Faith is
essential in this matter. My logic can make and
unmake innumerable hypotheses. An atheist might
floor me in a debate. But my faith runs so very
much faster than my reason that I can challenge
the whole world and say, 'God is, was and ever
shall be.'

But those who want to deny His existence are at
liberty to do so. He is merciful and compassionate.
He is not an earthly king needing an army to
make us accept His sway. He allows us freedom,

and yet His compassion commands obedience to His will. But if any one of us disdain to bow to His will, He says: 'So be it. My sun will shine no less for thee, my clouds will rain no less for thee. I need not force thee to accept my sway.' Of such a God let the ignorant dispute the existence. I am one of the millions of wise men who believe in Him and am never tired of bowing to Him and singing His glory.

Young India, 21-1-'26

4. TRUTH IS GOD

[Replying to a question asked of him at a meeting in Switzerland on his way back from the Round Table Conference in London, Gandhiji said :]

You have asked me why I consider that God is Truth. In my early youth I was taught to repeat what in Hindu scriptures are known as one thousand names of God. But these one thousand names of God were by no means exhaustive. We believe — and I think it is the truth — that God has as many names as there are creatures and, therefore we also say that God is nameless and since God has many forms we also consider Him formless, and since He speaks to us through many tongues we consider Him to be speechless and so on. And so when I came to study Islam I found that Islam too had many names for God. I would say with those who say God is Love, God is Love. But deep down in me I used to say that though God may be Love, God is Truth, above all. If it is possible for the human tongue to give the fullest description of God, I have come to the conclusion

that for myself, God is Truth. But two years ago I
went a step further and said that Truth is God.
You will see the fine distinction between the two
statements, viz. that God is Truth and Truth is
God. And I came to that conclusion after a
continuous and relentless search after Truth which
began nearly fifty years ago. I then found that the
nearest approach to Truth was through love. But I
also found that love has many meanings in the
English language at least and that human love in
the sense of passion could become a degrading
thing also. I found too that love in the sense of
Ahimsa had only a limited number of votaries in
the world. But I never found a double meaning in
connection with truth and even atheists had not
demurred to the necessity or power of truth. But in
their passion for discovering truth, the atheists
have not hesitated to deny the very existence of
God — from their own point of view rightly. And it
was because of this reasoning that I saw that
rather than say that God is Truth, I should say
that Truth is God. I recall the name of Charles
Bradlaugh who delighted to call himself an atheist,
but knowing as I do something of him, I would
never regard him as an atheist. I would call him a
God-fearing man, though I know that he would
reject the claim. His face would redden if I would
say "Mr. Bradlaugh, you are a truth-fearing man,
and so a God-fearing man." I would automatically
disarm his criticism by saying that Truth is God,
as I have disarmed criticisms of many a young
man. Add to this the great difficulty that millions
have taken the name of God and in His name
committed nameless atrocities. Not that scientists
very often do not commit cruelties in the name of

truth. I know how in the name of truth and science inhuman cruelties are perpetrated on animals when men perform vivisection. There are thus a number of difficulties in the way, no matter how you describe God. But the human mind is a limited thing, and you have to labour under limitations when you think of a being or entity who is beyond the power of man to grasp.

And then we have another thing in Hindu philosophy, viz. God alone is and nothing else exists, and the same truth you find emphasized and exemplified in the Kalma of Islam. There you find it clearly stated — that God alone is and nothing else exists. In fact the Sanskrit word for Truth is a word which literally means that which exists-*Sat*. For this and several other reasons that I can give you, I have come to the conclusion that the definition, 'Truth is God', gives me the greatest satisfaction. And when you want to find Truth as God the only inevitable means is Love, i.e. non-violence, and since I believe that ultimately the means and end are convertible terms, I should not hesitate to say that God is Love.

'What then is Truth ?'

A difficult question, but I have solved it for myself by saying that it is what the voice within tells you. How, then, you ask, different people think of different and contrary truths? Well, seeing that the human mind works through innumerable media and that the evolution of the human mind is not the same for all, it follows that what may be truth for one may be untruth for another, and hence those who have made these experiments have come to the conclusion that there are certain conditions to be observed in making those experiments. Just as for conducting scientific experiments there is an indispensable scientific course of instruction, in the same way strict preliminary discipline is necessary to qualify a person to make experiments in the spiritual realm. Every one should, therefore, realize his limitations before he speaks of his Inner Voice. Therefore we have the belief based upon experience, that those who would make individual search after Truth as God, must go through several vows, as for instance, the vow of truth, the vow of Brahmacharya (purity) – for you cannot possibly divide your love for Truth and God with anything else –, the vow of non-violence, of poverty and non-possession. Unless you impose on yourselves the five vows you may not embark on the experiment at all. There are several other conditions prescribed, but I must not take you through all of them. Suffice it to say that those who have made these experiments know that it is not proper for every one to claim to hear the voice of conscience, and it is because we have at the present moment everybody claiming the right of conscience without going through any discipline whatsoever and there is so much untruth being delivered to a bewildered world, all that I can, in true humility, present to you is that truth is not to be found by anybody who has not got an abundant sense of humility. If you would swim on the bosom of the ocean of Truth you must reduce yourself to a zero. Further than this I cannot go along this fascinating path.

Young India, 31-12-'31

5. GOD IS LOVE

Scientists tell us that without the presence of the cohesive force amongst the atoms that comprise this globe of ours, it would crumble to pieces and we cease to exist; and even as there is cohesive force in blind matter, so must there be in all things animate and the name for that cohesive force among animate beings is Love. We notice it between father and son, between brother and sister, friend and friend. But we have to learn to use that force among all that lives, and in the use of it consists our knowledge of God. Where there is love there is life; hatred leads to destruction.

Young India, 5-5-'20

Though there is enough repulsion in Nature, she *lives* by attraction. Mutual love enables Nature to persist. Man does not live by destruction. Self-love compels regard for others. Nations cohere because there is mutual regard among individuals composing them. Some day we must extend the national law to the universe, even as we have extended the family law to form nations – a larger family.

Young India, 2-3-'22

I have found that life persists in the midst of destruction and, therefore, there must be a higher law than that of destruction. Only under that law would a well-ordered society be intelligible and life worth-living. And if that is the law of life, we have

15

to work it out in daily life. Where-ever there are
jars, wherever you are confronted with an
opponent, conquer him with love. In this crude
manner, I have worked it out in my life. That does
not mean that all my difficulties are solved. Only I
have found that this law of love has answered as
the law of destruction has never done.

Young India, 1-10-'31

I believe that the sum total of the energy of
mankind is not to bring us down but to lift us up,
and that is the result of the definite, if
unconscious, working of the law of love. The fact
that mankind persists shows that the cohesive force
is greater than the disruptive force, centripetal
force greater than centrifugal.

Young India, 12-11-'31

If love or non-violence be not the law of our
being,.... there is no escape from a periodical
recrudescence of war, each succeeding one outdoing
the preceding one in ferocity.

Harijan, 26-9-'36

All the teachers that ever lived have preached
that law with more or less vigour. If love was not
the law of life, life would not have persisted in the
midst of death. Life is a perpetual triumph over
the grave. If there is a fundamental distinction
between man and beast, it is the former's progres-
sive recognition of the law and its application in
practice to his own personal life. All the saints of
the world, ancient and modern, were each
according to his light and capacity a living
illustration of that supreme law of our being. That
the brute in us seems so often to gain an easy
triumph is true enough. That, however, does not
disprove the law. It shows the difficulty of practice.

How should it be otherwise with a law which is as high as truth itself? When the practice of the law becomes universal, God will reign on earth as He does in Heaven. I need not be reminded that earth and Heaven are in us. We know the earth, we are strangers to the Heaven within us. If it is allowed that for some the practice of love is possible, it is arrogance not to allow even the possibility of its practice in all the others. Not very remote ancestors of ours indulged in cannibalism and many other practices which we would today call loathsome. No doubt in those days too there were Dick Sheppards who must have been laughed at and possibly pilloried for preaching the (to them) strange doctrine of refusing to eat fellow men.

Harijan, 26-9-'36

God is not a Power residing in the clouds. God is an unseen Power residing within us and nearer to us than finger-nails to the flesh. There are many powers lying hidden within us and we discover them by constant struggle. Even so may we find this Supreme Power if we make diligent search with the fixed determination to find Him. One such way is the way of Ahimsa. It is so very necessary because God is in every one of us and, therefore, we have to identify ourselves with every human being without exception. This is called cohesion or attraction in scientific language. In the popular language it is called love. It binds us to one another and to God. Ahimsa and love are one and the same thing.

From a private letter dated, 1-6-'42
Harijan, 28-3-'53

6.
GOD IS TRUTH – KNOWLEDGE – BLISS

The word Satya (Truth) is derived from Sat, which means 'being'. Nothing is or exists in reality except Truth. That is why Sat or Truth is perhaps the most important name of God. In fact it is more correct to say that Truth is God, than to say that God is Truth. But as we cannot do without a ruler or a general, such names of God as 'King of kings' or 'The Almighty' are and will remain generally current. On deeper thinking, however, it will be realized, that Sat or Satya is the only correct and fully significant name for God.

And where there is Truth, there also is knowledge which is true. Where there is no Truth, there can be no true Knowledge. That is why the word Chit or Knowledge is associated with the name of God. And where there is true Knowedge, there is always Bliss (Ananda). There sorrow has no place. And even as Truth is eternal, so is the Bliss derived from it. Hence we know God as Sat-Chit-Ananda, One who combines in Himself Truth, Knowledge and Bliss.

Devotion to this Truth is the sole justification for our existence. All our activities should be centred in Truth. Truth should be the very breath of our life. When once this stage in the pilgrim's progress is reached, all other rules of correct living will come without effort, and obedience to them will be

18

instinctive. But without Truth it is impossible to observe any principles or rules in life.

Generally speaking, observation of the law of Truth is understood merely to mean that we must speak the truth. But we in the Ashram should understand the word Satya or Truth in a much wider sense. There should be Truth in thought, Truth in speech, and Truth in action. To the man who has realized this Truth in its fulness, nothing else remains to be known, because all knowledge is necessarily included in it. What is not included in it is not Truth, and so not true knowledge; and there can be no inward peace without true knowledge. If we once learn how to apply this never-failing test of Truth, we will at once be able to find out what is worth doing, what is worth seeing, what is worth reading.

But how is one to realize this Truth, which may be likened to the philosopher's stone or the cow of plenty ? By single-minded devotion *(abhyasa)* and indifference to all other interests in life *(vairagya)*- replies the Bhagavad-gita. In spite, however, of such devotion, what may appear as truth to one person will often appear as untruth to another person. But that need not worry the seeker. Where there is honest effort, it will be realized that what appear to be different truths are like the countless and apparently different leaves of the same tree. Does not God Himself appear to different individuals in different aspects ? Still we know that He is one. But Truth is the right designation of God. Hence there is nothing wrong in every man following Truth according to his lights. Indeed it is his duty to do so. Then if there is a mistake on the part of anyone so following Truth, it will be automatically set right. For the quest of Truth involves *tapas* – self-suffering, sometimes even unto death. There can be no place in it for even a trace of self-interest. In such selfless search for Truth nobody can lose his bearings for long. Directly he takes to the wrong path he stumbles, and is thus redirected to the right path. Therefore the pursuit of Truth is true *bhakti* (devotion). It is the path that leads to God. There is no place in it for cowardice, no place for defeat. It is the talisman by which death itself becomes the portal to life eternal.

In this connection it would be well to ponder over the lives and examples of Harishchandra, Prahlad, Ramachandra, Imam Hasan and Imam Hussain, the Christian saints, etc. How beautiful it would be, if all of us, men and women, devoted ourselves wholly to Truth in all that we might do in our waking hours, whether working, eating, drinking, or playing, till dissolution of the body makes us one with Truth ? God as Truth has been for me a treasure beyond price: may He be so to every one of us.

From Yeravda Mandir, Chapter I.

7. GOD AND NATURE

We do not know all the laws of God nor their working. Knowledge of the tallest scientist or the greatest spiritualist is like a particle of dust. If God is not a personal being for me like my earthly father, He is infinitely more. He rules me in the tiniest detail of my life. I believe literally that not a leaf moves but by His will. Every breath I take depends upon His sufferance.

Harijan, 16-2-'34

He and His Law are one. The Law is God. Anything attributed to Him is not a mere attribute. He is the attribute. He is Truth, Love and Law and a million other things that human ingenuity can name.

Harijan, 16-2-'34

The laws of Nature are changeless, unchangeable, and there are no miracles in the sense of infringement or interruption of Nature's laws. But we limited beings fancy all kinds of things and impute our limitations to God. We may copy God, but not He us. We may not divide Time for Him. Time for Him is eternity. For us there is past, present and future. And what is human life of a hundred years but less than a mere speck in the eternity of Time?

Harijan, 17-4-'37

God Himself has reserved no right of revision of His own laws nor is there any need for Him for any such revision. He is all-powerful, all-knowing. He knows at the same time and without any effort the past, the present and the future. He has therefore nothing to reconsider, nothing to revise, nothing to alter and nothing to amend.

Young India, 25-11-'26

This earthly existence of ours is more brittle than the glass bangles that ladies wear. You can keep glass bangles for thousands of years if you treasure them in a chest and let them remain untouched. But this earthly existence is so fickle that it may be wiped out in the twinkling of an eye. Therefore, while we get breathing time, let us get rid of the distinctions of high and low, purify our hearts and be ready to face our Maker when an earthquake or some natural calamity or death in the ordinary course overtakes us.

Harijan, 2-2-'34

I share the belief with the whole world – civilized and uncivilized-that calamities (such as the Bihar earthquake of 1934) come to mankind as chastisement for their sins. When that conviction comes from the heart, people pray, repent and purify themselves.... I have but a limited knowledge of His purpose. Such calamities are not a mere caprice of the Deity or Nature. They obey fixed laws as surely as the planets move in obedience to laws governing their movement. Only we do not know the laws governing these events and, therefore, call them calamities or disturbances.

Harijan, 2-2-'34

There is a divine purpose behind every physical calamity. That perfected science will one day be able to tell us beforehand when earthquakes will occur, as it tells us today of eclipses, is quite possible. It will be another triumph of the human mind. But such triumph even indefinitely multiplied can bring about no purification of self without which nothing is of any value.

Harijan, 8-6-'35

I ask those who appreciate the necessity of inward purification to join in the prayer that we may read the purpose of God behind such visitations, that they may humble us and prepare us to face our Maker whenever the call comes, and that we may be ever ready to share the sufferings of our fellows whosoever they may be.

Harijan, 8-6-'35

To say that God permits evil in this world may

not be pleasing to the ear. But if He is held responsible for the good, it follows that He has to be responsible for the evil too. Did not God permit Ravana to exhibit unparalleled strength? Perhaps the root cause of the perplexity arises from a lack of the real understanding of what God is. God is not a person. He transcends description. He is the Lawmaker, the Law and the Executor. No human being can well arrogate these powers to himself. If he did, he would be looked upon as an unadulterated dictator. They become only Him whom we wroship as God.

Harijan, 24-2-'46

In a strictly scientific sense God is at the bottom of both good and evil. He directs the assassin's dagger no less than the surgeon's knife. But for all that good and evil are, for human purposes, from each other distinct and incompatible, being symbolical of light and darkness, God and Satan.

Harijan, 20-2-'37

I do not regard God as a person. Truth for me is God, and God's Law and God are not different things or facts, in the sense that an earthly king and his law are different. Because God is an idea, Law Himself. Therefore, it is impossible to conceive God as breaking the Law. He, therefore, does not rule our actions and withdraw Himself. When we say He rules our actions, we are simply using human language and we try to limit Him. Otherwise He and His Law abide everywhere and govern everything. Therefore, I do not think that He answers in every detail every request of ours, but there is no doubt that He rules our action, and I literally believe that not a blade of grass grows or moves without His will. The free will we enjoy is

less than that of a passenger on a crowded deck.
"Do you feel a sense of freedom in your
communion with God?"

I do. I do not feel cramped as I would on a boat
full of passengers. Although I know that my
freedom is less than that of a passenger, I
appreciate that freedom as I have imbibed through
and through the central teaching of the Gita that
man is the maker of his own destiny in the sense
that he has freedom of choice as to the manner in
which he uses that freedom. But he is no controller
of results. The moment he thinks he is, he comes
to grief.

Harijan 23-3-'40

8. GOD AS DARIDRANARAYAN

Daridranarayan is one of the millions of names
by which humanity knows God who is unnameable
and unfathomable by human understanding and it
means God of the poor, God appearing in the
hearts of the poor.

Young India, 4-4-'29

For the poor the economic is the spiritual. You
cannot make any other appeal to those starving
millions. It will fall flat on them. But you take food
to them and they will regard you as their God.
They are incapable of any other thought.

Young India, 5-5-'27

With this very hand I have collected soiled pies
from them tied tightly in their rags. Talk to them
of modern progress. Insult them by taking the
name of God before them in vain. They will call
you and me fiends if we talk about God to them.

They know, if they know God at all, a God of terror, vengeance, a pitiless tyrant.

Young India, 15-9-'27

I dare not take before them the message of God. I may as well place before the dog over there the message of God as before those hungry millions who have no lustre in their eyes and whose only God is their bread. I can take before them a message of God only by taking the message of sacred work before them. It is good enough to talk of God whilst we are sitting here after a nice breakfast and looking forward to a nicer luncheon, but how am I to talk of God to the millions who have to go without two meals a day? To them God can only appear as bread and butter. Well, the peasants of India were getting their bread from their soil. I offered them the spinning wheel in order that they may get butter and if I appear today ... in my loin-cloth it is because I come as the sole representative of those half-starved, half-naked dumb millions.

Young India, 15-10-'31

I claim to know my millions. All the hours of the day I am with them. They are my first care and last because I recognize no God except that God that is to be found in the hearts of the dumb millions. They do not recognize His presence; I do. And I worship the God that is Truth or Truth which is God through the service of these millions.

Harijan, 11-3-'39

I suggest that we are thieves in a way. If I take anything that I do not need for my own immediate use and keep it, I thieve it from somebody else. It is the fundamental law of Nature, without exception, that Nature produces enough for our

wants from day to day; and if only everybody took
enough for himself and nothing more, there would
be no pauperism in this world, there would be no
man dying of starvation.

Mahatma Gandhi (1918), p.189

In India we have got many millions of people
who have to be satisfied with one meal a day and
that meal consisting of a Chapati containing no fat
in it and a pinch of salt. You and I have no right
to anything that we really have until these millions
are clothed and fed. You and I ought to know
better, must adjust our wants, and even undergo
voluntary privation in order that they may be
nursed, fed and clothed.

Mahatma Gandhi (1918), p.189

9. THE VOICE OF GOD

My claim to hear the voice of God is no new
claim. Unfortunately there is no way that I know
of proving the claim except through results. God
will not be God if He allowed Himself to be an
object of proof by His creatures. But He does give
His willing slave the power to pass through the
fieriest of ordeals. I have been a willing slave to
this, most exacting Master for more than half a
century. His voice has been increasingly audible as
years have rolled By. He has never forsaken me
even in my darkest hour. He has saved me often
against myself and left me not a vestige of
independence. The greater the surrender to Him,
the greater has been my joy.

Harijan, 6-5-'33

Nobody has to my knowledge questioned the

possibility of the Inner Voice speaking to some, and it is a gain to the world even if one person's claim to speak under the authority of the Inner Voice can be really sustained. Many men make the claim, but not all will be able to substantiate it. But, it cannot and aught not to be suppressed for the sake of preventing false claimants. There is no danger whatsoever if many people could truthfully represent the Inner Voice. But, unfortunately, there is no remedy against hypocrisy. Virtue must not be suppressed because many will feign it. Men have always been found throughout the world claiming to speak for the Inner Voice. But no harm has yet overtaken the world through their shortlived activities. Before one is able to listen to that Voice, one has to go through a long and fairly severe course of training, and when it is the Inner Voice that speaks, it is unmistakable. The world cannot be successfully fooled for all time. There is, therefore, no danger of anarchy setting in because a humble man like me will not be suppressed and will dare to claim the authority of the Inner Voice, when he believes that he has heard it.

Harijan, 18-3-'33

For me the Voice of God, of Conscience, of Truth or the Inner Voice or 'the still small Voice' mean one and the same thing. I saw no form. I have never tried, for I have always believed God to be without form. But what I did hear was like a Voice from afar and yet quite near. It was as unmistakable as some human voice definitely speaking to me, and irresistible. I was not dreaming at the time I heard the Voice. The hearing of the Voice was preceded by a terrific struggle within me. Suddenly the Voice came upon me. I listened, made certain that it was the Voice, and the struggle ceased. I was calm. The determination was made accordingly, the date and the hour of the fast were fixed. Joy came over me. This was between 11 and 12 midnight. I felt refreshed and began to write the note about it which the reader must have seen.

Harijan, 8-7-'33

Could I give any further evidence that it was truly the Voice that I heard and that it was not an echo of my own heated imagination ? I have no further evidence to convince the sceptic. He is free to say that it was all self-delusion or hallucination. It may well have been so. I can offer no proof to the contrary. But I can say this-that not the unanimous verdict of the whole world against me could shake me from the belief that what I heard was the true Voice of God.

Harijan, 8-7-'33

But some think that God Himself is a creation of our own imagination. If that view holds good, then nothing is real, everything is of our own imagination. Even so, whilst my imagination dominates me, I can only act under its spell. Realest things are only relatively so. For me the Voice was more real than my own existence. It has never failed me, and for that matter, any one else.

Harijan, 8-7-'33

And every one who wills can hear the Voice. It is within every one. But like everything else, it requires previous and definite preparation.

Harijan, 8-7-'33

There is no question of hallucination. I have stated a simple scientific truth, thus to be tested by all who have the will and the patience to acquire the necessary qualifications, which are again incredibly simple to understand and easy enough to acquire where there is determination. I can only say : "You have to believe no one but yourselves. You must try to listen to the Inner Voice, but if you won't have the expression 'Inner Voice', you may use the expression 'dictates of reason', which you should obey, and if you will not parade God, I have no doubt you will parade something else which in the end will prove to be God, for fortunately, there is no one and nothing else but God in this universe." I would also submit that it is not every one claiming to act on the urge of the Inner Voice (who has that urge. After all, like every other faculty, this faculty for listening to the still small Voice within requires previous effort and training, perhaps much greater than what is required for the acquisition of any other faculty, and even if out of thousands of claimants only a few succeed in establishing their claim, it is well worth running the risk of having and tolerating doubtful claimants. A person falsely claiming to act under divine inspiration or the promptings of the Inner Voice without having any such, will fare worse than the one falsely claiming to act under the authority of an earthly sovereign. Whereas the latter on being exposed will escape with injury to his body the former may perish body and soul together. Charitable critics impute no fraud to me, but suggest that I am highly likely to be acting under some hallucination. The result for me, even then, will not be far different from what it would be if I was laying a false claim. A humble seeker that I claim to be has need to be most cautious and, to preserve the balance of mind, he has to reduce himself to zero before God will guide him. Let me not labour this point.

The Bombay Chronicle, 18-11-'33

10. GOD-REALIZATION

For me Truth is the sovereign principle, which includes numerous other principles. This Truth is not only truthfulness in word, but truthfulness in •thought also, and not only the relative truth of our conception, but the Absolute Truth, the Eternal Principle, that is God. There are innumerable definitions of God, because His manifestations are innumerable. They overwhelm me with wonder and awe and for a moment stun me. But I worship God as Truth only. I have not yet found Him, but I am seeking after Him. I am prepared to sacrifice the things dearest to me in pursuit of this quest. Even if the sacrifice demanded be my very life I hope I may be prepared to give it. But as long as I have not realized this Absolute Truth, so long must I hold by the relative truth as I have conceived it. That relative truth must, meanwhile, be my beacon, my shield and buckler. Though this path is strait and narrow and sharp as the razor's edge, for me it has been the quickest and easiest. Even my Himalayan blunders have seemed trifling to me because I have kept strictly to this path. For the path has saved me from coming to grief, and I have gone forward according to my light. Often in my progress I have had faint glimpses of the Absolute Truth, God, and daily the conviction is growing upon me that He alone is real and all else is unreal.

Autobiography, (1948) pp.6-7

The further conviction has been growing upon me that whatever is possible for me is possible even for a child, and I have found sound reasons for saying so. The instruments for the quest of Truth are as simple as they are difficult. They may appear quite impossible to an arrogant person, and quite possible to an innocent child. The seeker after Truth should be humbler than the dust. The world crushes the dust under its feet, but the seeker after Truth should so humble himself that even the dust could crush him. Only then, and not till then, will he have a glimpse of Truth.

Autobiography, (1948,) pp.6-7

This belief in God has to be based on faith which transcends reason. Indeed; even the so-called realization has at bottom an element of faith without which it cannot be sustained. In the very nature of things it must be so. Who can transgress the limitations of his being? I hold that complete realization is impossible in this embodied life. Nor is it necessary. A living immovable faith is all that is required for reaching the full spiritual height attainable by human beings. God is not outside this earthly case of ours. Therefore, exterior proof is not of much avail, if any at all. We must ever fail to perceive Him through the senses, because He is beyond them. We can feel Him, if we will. but withdraw ourselves from the senses. The divine music is incessantly going on within ourselves, but the loud senses drown the delicate music, which is unlike an infinitely superior to anything we can perceive or hear with our senses.

Harijan, 13-6-'36

I have seen and believe that God never appears to you in person, but in action which can only

account for your deliverance in your darkest hour.
Harijan, 13-6-'36

My uniform experience has convinced me that
there is no other God than Truth.... The little
fleeting glimpses... that I have been able to have of
Truth can hardly convey an idea of the
indescribable lustre of Truth, a million times more
intense than that of the sun we daily see with our
eyes. In fact, what I have caught is only the
faintest glimmer of that mighty effulgence. But this
much I can say with assurance as a result of all
my experiments, that a perfect vision of Truth can
only follow a complete realization of Ahimsa.
Young India, 7-2-'29

I have no special revelation of God's will. My
firm belief is that He reveals Himself daily to every
human being but we shut our ears to the still
small Voice. We shut our eyes to the Pillar of Fire
in front of us. I realize His omnipresence.
Young India, 25-5-'21

Man's ultimate aim is the realization of God,
and all his activities, social, political, religious,
have to be guided by the ultimate aim of the
vision of God. The immediate service of all
human beings becomes a necessary part of the
endeavour, simply because the only way to find
God is to see Him in his creation and be one
with it. This can only be done by service of all.
I am a part and parcel of the whole and I cannot
find Him apart from the rest of humanity. My
countrymen are my nearest neighbours. They
have become so help-less, so resourceless, so
inert that I must concentrate myself on serving
them. If I could persuade myself that I could
find Him in a Himalayan cave I would proceed

there immediately. But I know that I cannot find Him apart from humanity.

Harijan, 29-8-'36

The impenetrable darkness that surrounds us is not a curse but a blessing. He has given us power to see only the step in front of us, and it should be enough if Heavenly light reveals that step to us. We can then sing with Newman, 'One step enough for me'. And we may be sure from our past experience that the next step will always be in view. In other words, the impenetrable darkness is nothing so impenetrable as we imagine. But it seems impenetrable when, in our impatience, we want to look beyond that one step.

Harijan, 20-4-'34

I am surer of His existence than of the fact that you and I are sitting in this room. Then I can also testify that I may live without air and water but not without Him. You may pluck out my eyes, but that cannot kill me. You may chop off my nose, but that will not kill me. But blast my belief in God, and I am dead. You may call this a superstition, but I confess it is a superstition that I hug, even as I used to do the name of Rama in my childhood when there was any cause of danger or alarm. That was what an old nurse had taught me.

Harijan, 14-5-'38

God is the hardest taskmaster I have known on earth, and he tries you through and through. And when you find that your faith is failing or your body is failing you, and you are sinking, He comes to your assistance somehow or other and proves to you that you must not lose faith and that He is always at your beck and call, but on His terms, not on your terms. So I have found. I cannot recall a single instance when, at the eleventh hour, He has forsaken me.

Speeches and Writings of Mahatma Gandhi (1933), p.1069

11. THE PATH OF AHIMSA

The path of Truth is as narrow as it is straight. Even so is that of Ahimsa. It is like balancing oneself on the edge of a sword. By concentration an acrobat can walk on a rope. But the concentration required to tread the path of Truth and Ahimsa is far greater. The slightest inattention brings one tumbling to the ground. One can realize Truth and Ahimsa only by ceaseless striving....

Ahimsa is not the crude thing it has been made to appear. Not to hurt any living things is no doubt a part of Ahimsa. But it is its least expression. The principle of Ahimsa is hurt by every evil thought, by undue haste, by lying, by hatred, by wishing ill to anybody. It is also violated by our holding on to what the world needs. But the world needs even what we eat day by day. In the place where we stand there are millions of a micro-organisms to whom the place belongs, and who are hurt by our presence there. What should we do then? Should we commit suicide? Even that is no solution, if we believe, as we do, that so long as the spirit is attached to the flesh, on every destruction of body it weaves for itself another. The body will cease to be only when we give up all attachment to it. This freedom from all attachment is the realization of God as Truth. Such realization cannot be attained in a hurry. The body does not belong to us. While it lasts we must use it as a trust handed over to our charge. Treating in this way the things of the flesh, we may one day expect to become free from the burden of the body. Realizing the limitations of the flesh, we must strive day by day towards the ideal with what strength we have in us.

It is perhaps clear from the foregoing, that without Ahimsa it is not possible to seek and find Truth.

Ahimsa and Truth are so interwined that it is practically impossible to disentangle and separate them. They are like the two sides of a coin, or rather of a smooth unstamped metallic disc. Who can say, which is the obverse, and which is the reverse? Nevertheless, Ahimsa is the means; Truth is the end. Means to be means must always be within our reach, and so Ahimsa is our supreme duty. If we take care of the means, we are bound to reach the end sooner or later. When once we have grasped this point, final victory is beyond question. Whatever difficulties we encounter, whatever apparent reverses we sustain, we may not give up the quest for Truth which alone is, being God Himself.

From Yeravda Mandir, Chapter II

Non-violence is an active force of the highest order. It is soul-force or the power of Godhead within us. Imperfect man cannot grasp the whole of that essence-he would not be able to bear its full blaze, but even an infinitesimal fraction of it, when it becomes active within us, can work wonders. The sun in the heavens fills the whole universe with its life-giving warmth. But if one went too near it, it would consume him to ashes. Even so, it is with Godhead. We become Godlike to the extent we realize non-violence, but we can never become wholly God. Non-violence is like radium in its action. An infinitesimal quantity of it embedded in a malignant growth, acts continuously, silently and ceaselessly till it has transformed the whole mass of the diseased tissue into a healthy one. Similarly, even a little of true non-violence acts in a silent, subtle, unseen way and leavens the whole society.

Harijan, 12-11-'38

Truth without humility would be an arrogant caricature. He who wants to practise truth knows how hard it is. The world may applaud his so-called triumphs. Little does the world know his falls. A truthful man is a chastened being. He has need to be humble. A man who wants to love the whole world including one who calls himself his enemy knows how impossible it is to do so in his own strength. He must be as mere dust before he can understand the elements of Ahimsa. He is nothing if he does not daily grow in humility as he grows in love.... And no one can see God face to face who has aught of the I in him. He must become a cypher if he would see God. Who shall dare say in this storm-tossed universe, 'I have won'? God triumphs in us, never we.... What is true of the physical world is true of the spiritual. If in order to gain a worldly battle, Europe sacrificed several million lives during the late war, itself a transitory event, what wonder that in the spiritual battle millions have to perish in the attempt so that one complete example may be left to the world?

Young India, 25-6-'25

Non-violence is the greatest force at the disposal of mankind. It is mightier than the mightiest

THE PATH OF AHIMSA

weapon of destruction devised by the ingenuity of man. Destruction is not the law of the humans. Man lives freely by his readiness to die, if need be, at the hands of his brother, never by killing him. Every murder or injury, no matter for what cause, committed or inflicted on another is a crime against humanity.

Harijan, 20-7-'35

The virtues of mercy, non-violence, love and truth in any man can be truly tested only when they are pitted against ruthlessness, violence, hate and untruth.

If this is true, then it is incorrect to say that Ahimsa is of no avail before a murderer. It can certainly be said that to experiment with Ahimsa in face of a murderer is to seek self-destruction. But this is the real test of Ahimsa. He who gets himself killed out of sheer helplessness, however, can in no wise be said to have passed the test. He who when being killed bears no anger against this murderer and even asks God to forgive him is truly non-violent. History relates this of Jesus Christ. With his dying breath on his cross, he is reported to have said : "Father, forgive them for they know not what they do." We can get similar instances from other religions but the quotation is given because it is world famous.

It is another matter that our non-violence has not reached such heights. It would be wholly wrong for us to lower the standard of Ahimsa by reason of our own fault or lack of experience. Without true understanding of the ideal, we can never hope to reach it. It is necessary for us, therefore, to apply our reason to understand the power of non-violence.

Harijan, 28-4-'46

Ahimsa is a comprehensive principle. We are helpless mortals caught in the conflagration of Himsa. The saying that life lives on life has a deep meaning in it. Man cannot for a moment live without consciously or unconsciously committing outward Himsa. The very fact of his living, eating, drinking and moving about necessarily involves some Himsa, destruction of life, be it ever so minute. A votary of Ahimsa therefore remains true to his faith if the spring of all his actions is compassion, if he shuns to the best of his ability the destruction of the tiniest creature, tries to save it, and thus incessantly strives to be free from the deadly coil of Himsa. He will be constantly growing in self-restraint and compassion, but he can never become entirely free from outward Himsa.

Autobiography (1948), pp. 427-28

Then again, because underlying Ahimsa is the unity of all life, the error of one cannot but affect all, and hence man cannot be wholly free from Himsa. So long as he continues to be a social being, he cannot but participate in the Himsa that the very existence of society involves. When two nations are fighting, the duty of a votary of Ahimsa is to stop the war. He who is not equal to that duty, he who has no power of resisting war, he who is not qualified to resist war, may take part in war, and yet whole-heartedly try to free himself, his nation and the world from war.

Autobiography (1948), p.428

12.
PRAYER – THE ESSENCE OF RELIGION

I believe that prayer is the very soul and essence of religion, and therefore prayer must be the very core of the life of man, for no man can live without religion. There are some who in the egotism of their reason declare that they have nothing to do with religion. But it is like a man saying that he breathes but that he has no nose. Whether by reason, or by instinct, or by superstition, man acknowledges some sort of relation-ship with the divine. The rankest agnostic or atheist does acknowledge the need of a moral principle, and associates something good with its observance and something bad with its non-observance. Bradlaugh, whose atheism is well known, always insisted on proclaiming his innermost conviction. He had to suffer a lot for thus speaking the truth, but he delighted in it and said that truth is its own reward. Not that he was quite insensible to the joy resulting from the observance of truth. This joy however is not all worldly, but springs out of communion with the divine. That is why I have said that even a man who disowns religion cannot and does not live without religion.

Now I come to the next thing, viz. that prayer is the very core of man's life, as it is the most vital part of religion. Prayer is either petitional or in its wider sense is inward communion. In either case

the ultimate result is the same. Even when it is
petitional, the petition should be for the cleansing
and purification of the soul, for freeing it from the
layers of ignorance and darkness that envelop it.
He therefore who hungers for the awakening of the
divine in him must fall back on prayer. But prayer
is no mere exercise of words or of the ears, it is no
mere repetition of empty formula. Any amount of
repetition of Ramanama is futile if it fails to stir
the soul. It is better in prayer to have a heart
without words than words without a heart. It must
be in clear response to the spirit which hungers for
it. And even as a hungry man relishes a hearty
meal, a hungry soul will relish a heartfelt prayer.
And I am giving you a bit of my experience and
that of my companions when I say that he who has
experienced the magic of prayer may do without
food for days together but not a single moment
without prayer. For without prayer there is no
inward peace.

If that is the case, someone will say, we should
be offering our prayers every minute of our lives.
There is no doubt about it, but we erring mortals,
who find it difficult to retire within ourselves for
inward communion even for a single moment, will
find it impossible to remain perpetually in
communion with the divine. We therefore fix some
hours when we make a serious effort to throw off
the attachments of the world for a while, we make
a serious endeavour to remain, so to say, out of the
flesh. You have heard Surdas's hymn. It is the
passionate cry of a soul hungering for union with
the divine. According to our standards he was a
saint, but according to his own he was a
proclaimed sinner. Spiritually he was miles ahead

of us, but he felt the separation from the divine so keenly that he has uttered that anguished cry* in lothing and despair.

I have talked of the necessity for prayer, and therethrough I have dealt with the essence of prayer. We are born to serve our fellowmen, and we cannot properly do so unless we are wide awake. There is an eternal struggle raging in man's breast between the powers of darkness and of light, and he who has not the sheet-anchor of prayer to rely upon will be a victim to the powers of darkness. The man of prayer will be at peace with himself and with the whole world; the man who goes about the affairs of the world without a prayerful heart will be miserable and will make the world also miserable. Apart therefore from its bearing on man's condition after death, prayer has incalculable value for man in this world of the living. Prayer is the only means of bringing about orderliness and peace and repose in our daily acts. Take care of the vital thing and other things will take care of themselves. Rectify one angle of a square, and the other angles will be automatically right.

Begin therefore your day with prayer, and make it so soulful that it may remain with you until the evening. Close the day with prayer so that you may have a peaceful night free from dreams and nightmares. Do not worry about the form of prayer. let it be any form, it should be such as can put us into communion with the divine. Only, whatever be the form, let not the spirit wander while the words

* मो सम कौन कुटिल खल कामी ।

'Who is so corrupt, wicked and lustful as I !'

of prayer run on out of your mouth.

All things in the universe, including the sun and the moon and the stars, obey certain laws. Without the restraining influence of these laws the world would not go on for a single moment. You, whose mission in life is service of your fellowmen, will go to pieces if you do not impose on yourselves some sort of discipline, and prayer is a necessary spiritual discipline. It is discipline and restraint that separates us from the brute. If we will be men walking with our heads erect and not walking on all fours, let us understand and put ourselves under voluntary discipline and restraint.

Young India, 23-1-'30

13. WHY PRAY?

Why pray at all? Does not God, if there be One, know what has happened? Does He stand in need of prayer to enable Him to do His duty?

No, God needs no reminder. He is within every one. Nothing happens without His permission. Our prayer is a heart search. It is a reminder to ourselves that we are helpless without His support. No effort is complete without prayer, − without a definite recognition that the best human endeavour is of no effect if it has not God's blessing behind it. Prayer is a call to humility. It is a call to self-purification, to inward search.

Harijan, 8-6-'35

In my opinion, Rama, Rahaman, Ahurmazda, God or Krishna are all attempts on the part of man to name that invisible force which is the greatest of all forces. It is inherent in man, imperfect though he be, ceaselessly to strive after perfection. In the attempt he falls into reverie. And, just as a child tries to stand, falls down again and again and ultimately learns how to walk, even so man, with all his intelligence, is a mere infant as compared to the infinite and ageless God. This may appear to be an exaggeration but is not. Man can only describe God in his own poor language. The power we call God defies description. Nor does that power stand in need of any human effort to describe Him. It is man who requires the means whereby he can describe that power which is vaster than the ocean. If this premise is accepted, there is no need to ask why we pray. Man can only conceive God within the limitations of his own mind. If God is vast and boundless as the ocean, how can a tiny drop like man imagine what He is? He can only experience what the ocean is like, if he falls into and is merged in it. This realization is beyond description. In Madame Blavatsky's language man, in praying, worships his own glorified self. He can truly pray, who has the conviction that God is within him. He who has not, need not pray. God will not be offended, but I can say from experience that he who does not pray is certainly a loser. What matters then whether one man worships God as a Person and another as Force? Both do right according to their lights. None knows and perhaps never will know what is the absolutely proper way to pray. The ideal must always remain the ideal. One need only remember that God is the Force among all the forces. All other forces are material. But God is the vital force or spirit which is all-pervading, all-embracing and therefore beyond human ken.

Harijan, 18-8-'46

A Dialogue with a Buddhist

Dr. Fabri, a follower of Buddha, called on Gandhiji at Abbottabad, and enquired :

"Gould the Divine Mind be changed by prayer? Could one find it out by prayer?"

"It is a difficult thing to explain fully what I do when I pray," said Gandhiji. "But I must try to answer your question. The Divine Mind is unchangeable, but that Divinity is in everyone and everything – animate and inanimate. The meaning of prayer is that I want to evoke that Divinity within me. Now I may have that intellectual conviction, but not a living touch. And so when I pray for Swaraj or Independence for India I pray or wish for adequate power to gain that Swaraj or to make the largest contribution I can towards winning it, and I maintain that I can get that power in answer to prayer."

"Then you are not justified in calling it prayer; to pray means to beg or demand," said Dr. Fabri.

"Yes, indeed. You may say I beg it of myself, of my Higher self, the Real self with which I have not yet achieved complete identification. You may, therefore, describe it as a continual longing to lose oneself in the Divinity which comprises all."

"What about the people who cannot pray?" asked Dr. Fabri.

"Be humble," said Gandhiji, "I would say to them, and do not limit even the real Buddha by your own conception of Buddha. He could not have ruled the lives of millions of men that he did and does today if he was not humble enough to pray. There is something infinitely higher than intellect that rules us and even the sceptics. Their scepticism and philosophy does not help them in critical periods of their lives. They need something better, something outside them that can sustain them. And so if someone puts a conundrum before me, I say to him, "You are not going to know the meaning of God or prayer unless you reduce yourself to a cipher. You must be humble enough to see that in spite of your greatness and gigantic intellect you are but a speck in the universe. A merely intellectual conception of the things of life is not enough. It is the spiritual conception which eludes the intellect, and which alone can give one satisfaction. Even moneyed men have critical periods in their lives. Though they are surrounded by everything that money can buy and affection can give, they find themselves at certain moments in their lives utterly distracted. It is in these moments that we have a glimpse of God, a vision of Him who is guiding every one of our steps in life. It is prayer.' "

"You mean what we might call a true religious experience which is stronger than intellectual conception," said Dr. Fabri. "Twice in life I had that experience, but I have since lost it. But I now find great comfort in one or two sayings of Buddha : 'Selfishness is the cause of sorrow', and 'Remember, monks, everything is fleeting'. To think of these takes almost the place of belief."

"That is prayer," repeated Gandhiji with an insistence that could not but have gone home.

Harijan, 19-8-'39

14.
HOW, TO WHOM AND WHEN TO PRAY

'Often, Sir, do you ask us to worship God, to pray but never tell us how to and to whom to do so. Will you kindly enlighten me?' asks a reader of the *Navajivan*. Worshipping God is singing the praise of God. Prayer is a confession of one's unworthiness and weakness. God has a thousand names, or rather, He is Nameless. We may worship or pray to Him by whichever name that pleases us. Some call Him Rama, some Krishna, others call Him Rahim, and yet others call Him God. All worship the same spirit, but as all foods do not agree with all, all names do not appeal to all. Each chooses the name according to his associations, and He being the In-Dweller, All-Powerful and Omniscient knows our innermost feelings and responds to us according to our deserts.

Worship or prayer, therefore, is not to be performed with the lips, but with the heart. And that is why it can be performed equally by the dumb and the stammerer, by the ignorant and the stupid. And the prayers of those whose tongues are nectared but whose hearts are full of poison are never heard. He, therefore, who would pray to God, must cleanse his heart. Rama was not only on the lips of Hunuman, He was enthroned in his heart. He gave Hanuman exhaustless strength. In His strength he lifted the mountain and crossed the ocean. It is faith that steers us through stormy seas, faith that moves mountains and faith that jumps across the ocean. That faith is nothing but a living, wideawake consciousness of God within. He who has achieved that faith wants nothing. Bodily diseased he is spiritually healthy, physically pure, he rolls in spiritual riches.

'But how is the heart to be cleansed to this extent?' one might well ask. The language of the lips is easily taught; but who can teach the language of the heart ? Only the *bhakta* – the true devotee – knows it and can teach it. The Gita has defined the *bhakta* in three places and talked of him generally everywhere. But a knowledge of the definition of a *bhakta* is hardly a sufficient guide. They are rare on this earth. I have therefore suggested the Religion of Service as the means. God of Himself seeks for His seat the heart of him who serves his fellowmen. That is why Narasinha Mehta who 'saw and knew' sang 'He is a true *Vaishnava* who knows to melt at other's woe.' Such was Abu Ben Adhem. He served his fellowmen, and therefore his name topped the list of those who served God.

But who are the suffering and the woebegone? The suppressed and the poverty-stricken. He who would be a *bhakta,* therefore, must serve these by body, soul and mind. How can he who regards the 'suppressed' classes as untouchables serve them by the body? He who does not even condescend to exert his body to the extent of spinning for the sake of the poor, and trots out lame excuses, does not know the meaning of service. An able-bodied wretch deserves no alms, but an appeal to work for his bread. Alms debase him. He who spins before

the poor inviting them to do likewise serves God as
no one else does. 'He who gives Me even a trifle
such as a fruit or a flower or even a leaf in the
spirit of *bhakti* is My servant,' says the Lord in the
Bhagawadgita. And He hath his footstool where
live the humble, the lowliest and the lost.'
Spinning, therefore, for such is the greatest prayer,
the greatest worship, the greatest sacrifice.

"Prayer, therefore, may be done by any name. A
prayerful heart is the vehicle and service makes
the heart prayerful. Those Hindus who in this age
serve the untouchables from a full heart truly pray;
the Hindus and those others who spin prayerfully
for the poor and the indigent truly pray.

Young India, 24-9-'25

There can be no fixed rule laid down as to the
time these devotional acts should take. It depends
upon individual temperament. These are precious
moments in one's daily life. The exercises are
intended to sober and humble us and enable us to
realize that nothing happens without His will and
that we are but 'clay in the hands of the Potter'.
These are moments when one reviews one's
immediate past, confesses one's weaknesses, asks
for forgiveness and strength to be and do better.
One minute may be enough for some, twenty-four
hours may be too little for others. For those who
are filled with the presence of God in them, to
labour is to pray. Their life is one continuous
prayer or act of worship. For those others who act
only to sin, to indulge themselves, and live for self,
no time is too much. If they had patience and faith
and the will to be pure, they would pray till they
feel the definite purifying presence of God within
them. For us ordinary mortals there must be a

middle path between these two extremes. We are not so exalted as to be able to say that all our acts are a dedication, nor perhaps are we so far gone as to be living purely for self. Hence have all religions set apart times for general devotion. Unfortunately these have now-a-days become merely mechanical and formal, where they are not hypocritical. What is necessary is the correct attitude to accompany these devotions.

For definite personal prayer in the sense of asking God for something, it should certainly be in one's own tongue.

Nothing can be grander than to ask God to make us act justly towards everything that lives.

Young India, 10-6-'26

15 FASTS

A genuine fast cleanses body, mind and soul. It crucifies the flesh and to that extent sets the soul free. A sincere prayer can work wonders. It is an intense longing of the soul for its even greater purity. Purity thus gained when it is utilized for a noble purpose becomes a prayer. The mundane use of the Gayatri, its repetition for healing the sick, illustrates the meaning we have given to prayer. When the same Gayatri *japa* is performed with a humble and concentrated mind in an intelligent manner in times of national difficulties and calamities, it becomes a most potent instrument for warding off danger. There can be no greater mistake than to suppose that the recitation of the Gayatri, the Namaz or the Christian prayer are superstitions fit to be practised by the ignorant and the credulous. Fasting and prayer therefore are a most powerful process of purification and that which purifies necessarily enables us the better to do our duty and to attain our goal. If therefore fasting and prayer seem at times not to answer, it is not because there is nothing in them but because the right spirit is not behind them.

A man who fasts and gambles away the whole of the day as do so many on Janmashtami day, naturally, not only obtains no result from the fast in the shape of greater purity but such a dissolute fast leaves him on the contrary degraded. A fast to be true must be accompanied by readiness to receive pure thoughts and determination to resist all Satan's temptations. Similarly a prayer to be true has to be intelligible and definite. One has to identify oneself with it. Counting beads with the name of Allah on one's lips whilst the mind wanders in all directions is worse than useless.

Young India, 24-3-'20

Of course, it is not to be denied that fasts can be really coercive. Such are fasts to attain a selfish object. A fast undertaken to wring money from a person or for fulfilling some such personal end would amount to the exercise of coercion or undue influence. I would unhesitatingly advocate resistance of such undue influence. I have myself successfully resisted it in the fasts that have been undertaken or threatened against me. And if it is argued that the dividing line between a selfish and an unselfish end is often very thin, I would urge that a person who regards the end of a fast to be selfish or otherwise base should resolutely refuse to yield to it, even though the refusal may result in the death of the fasting person. If people will cultivate the habit of disregarding fasts which in their opinion are taken for unworthy ends, such fasts will be robbed of the taint of coercion and undue influence. Like all human institutions, fasting can be both legitimately and illegitimately used. But as a great weapon in the armoury of Satyagraha, it cannot be given up because of its possible abuse. Satyagraha has been designed as an effective substitute for violence. This use is in its infancy and, therefore, not yet perfected. But as the author of modern Satyagraha I cannot give up any of its manifold uses without forfeiting my claim to handle it in the spirit of a humble seeker.

Harijan, 9-9-'33

Christian Objections

[With reference to a letter from C. F. Andrews expressing moral repulsion amongst Christians in England against 'fasting unto death', Gandhiji wrote:]

Hindu religious literature is replete with instances of fasting, and thousands of Hindus fast even today on the slightest pretext. It is the one thing that does the least harm. There is no doubt that, like everything that is good, fasts are abused. That is inevitable. One cannot forbear to do good, because sometimes evil is done under its cover.

My real difficulty is with my Christian Protestant friends, of whom I have so many and whose friendship I value beyond measure. Let me confess to them that, though from my very first contact with them I have known their dislike for fasts, I have never been able to understand it.

Mortification of the flesh has been held all the world over as a condition of spiritual progress. There is no prayer without fasting, taking fasting in its widest sense. A complete fast is a complete and literal denial of self. It is the truest prayer. "Take my life and let it be always, only, all for Thee" is not, should not be, a mere lip or figurative expression. It has to be a reckless and joyous giving without the least reservation. Abstention from food and even water is but the mere beginning, the least part of the surrender.

Whilst I was putting together my thoughts for this article, a pamphlet written by Christians came into my hands wherein was a chapter on the necessity of example rather than precept. In this occurs a quotation from the 3rd Chapter of Jonah. The prophet had foretold that Nineveh, the great city, was to be destroyed on the fortieth day of his entering it:

"So the people of Nineveh believed God, and proclaimed a fast, and put on sack-cloth, from the greatest of them even to the least of them. For word came unto the king of Nineveh, and he arose from his throne, and he laid his robe from him, and covered him with sack-cloth, and sat in ashes. And he caused it to be proclaimed and published through Nineveh by the decree of the king and the nobles saying, 'Let neither man nor beast, herd nor flock, taste anything; let them not feed, nor drink water. But let man and beast be covered with sack-cloth, and cry mightily unto God: yea, let them turn every one from his evil way, and from the violence that is in their hands. Who can tell if God will turn and repent, and turn away from his fierce anger, that we perish not?' And God saw their works, that they turned from their evil way; and God repented of the evil that he had said that he would do unto them; and he did it not."

Thus this was a 'fast unto death'. But every fast unto death is not suicide. This fast of the king and the people of Nineveh was a great and humble prayer to God for deliverance. It was to be either deliverance or death. Even so was my fast, if I may compare it to the Biblical fast. This chapter from the book of Jonah reads like an incident in the Ramayana.

Harijan, 15-4-'33

16. THE ETERNAL DUEL

Man's destined purpose is to conquer old habits, to overcome the evil in him and to restore good to its rightful place. If religion does not teach us how to achieve this conquest, it teaches us nothing. But there is no royal road to success in this the truest enterprise in life. Cowardice is perhaps the greatest vice from which we suffer and is also possibly the greatest violence, certainly far greater than bloodshed and the like that generally go under the name of violence. For it comes from want of faith in God and ignorance of His attributes.... But I can give my own testimony and say that a heartfelt prayer is undoubtedly the most potent instrument that man possesses for overcoming cowardice and all other bad old habits. Prayer is an impossibility without a living faith in the presence of God within.

Christianity and Islam describe the same process as a duel between God and Satan, not outside but within; Zoroastrianism as a duel between Ahurmazd and Ahriman; Hinduism as a duel

between forces of good and forces of evil. We have
to make our choice whether we should ally
ourselves with the forces of evil or with the forces
of good. And to pray to God is nothing but that
sacred alliance between God and man whereby he
attains his deliverance from the clutches of the
prince of darkness. But a heartfelt prayer is not a
recitation with the lips. It is a yearning from
within which expresses itself in every word, every
act, nay, every thought of man. When an evil
thought successfully assails him, he may know that
he has offered but a lip prayer and similarly with
regard to an evil word escaping his lips or an evil
act done by him. Real prayer is an absolute shield
and protection against this trinity of evils. Success
does not always attend the very first effort at such
real living prayer. We have to strive against
ourselves, we have to believe in spite of ourselves,
because months are as our years. We have
therefore to cultivate illimitable patience if we will
realize the efficacy of prayer. There will be
darkness, disappointment and even worse; but we
must have courage enough to battle against all
these and not succumb to cowardice. There is no
such thing as retreat for a man of prayer.

What I am relating is not a fairy tale. I have not
drawn an imaginary picture. I have summed up
the testimony of men who have by prayer
conquered every difficulty in their upward progress,
and I have added my own humble testimony that
the more I live the more I realize how much I owe
to faith and prayer which is one and the same
thing for me. And I am quoting an experience not
limited to a few hours, or days or weeks, but
extending over an unbroken period of nearly 40

years. I have had my share of disappointments, uttermost darkness, counsels of despair, counsels of caution, subtlest assaults of pride, but I am able to say that my faith, – and I know that it is still little enough, by no means as great as I want it to be, – has ultimately conquered every one of these difficulties up to now. If we have faith in us, if we have a prayerful heart, we may not tempt God, may not make terms with Him.... Not until we have reduced ourselves to nothingness can we conquer the evil in us. God demands nothing less than complete self-surrender as the price for the only real freedom that is worth having. And when a man thus loses himself, he immediately finds himself in the service of all that lives. It becomes his delight and his recreation. He is a new man never weary of spending himself in the service of God's creation.

Young India, 20-12-'28

17. SELF-PURIFICATION

love and Ahimsa are matchless in their effect. But, in their play there is no fuss, show, noise or placards. They presuppose self-confidence which in its turn presupposes self-purification. Men of stainless character and self-purification will easily inspire confidence and automatically purify the atmosphere around them.

Young India, 6-9-'28

Identification with everything that lives is impossible without self-purification; without self-purification the observance of the law of Ahimsa must remain an empty dream; God can never be realized by one who is not pure of heart. Self-purification, therefore, must mean purification in all the walks of life. And purification being highly infectious, purification of oneself necessarily leads to the purification of one's surroundings.

Autobiography, 1948; p.615

But the path of purification is hard and steep. To attain to perfect purity one has to become absolutely passion-free in thought, speech, and action; to rise above the opposing currents of love and hatred, attachment and repulsion. I know that I have not in me as yet that triple purity, in spite of constant, ceaseless striving for it. That is why the world's praise fails to move me, indeed it very often stings me. To conquer the subtle passions seems to me to be harder far than the physical conquest of the world by the force of arms.

Autobiography, (1948); p.616

Never own defeat in a sacred cause and make up your minds henceforth that you will be pure and that you will find a response from God. But God never answers the prayers of the arrogant, nor the prayers of those who bargain with Him. ... If you would ask Him to help you, you would go to Him in all your nakedness, approach Him without reservation, also without fear or doubts as to how He can help a fallen being like you. He who helped millions who have approached Him, is He going to desert you ? He makes no exceptions whatsoever and you will find that every one of your prayers will be answered. The prayer of even the most impure will be answered. I am telling you this out of my personal experience, I have gone through the purgatory. Seek first the Kingdom of Heaven and everything will be added unto you.

Young India, 4-4-'29

18. VALUE OF SILENCE

It has often occurred to me that a seeker after truth has to be silent. I know the wonderful efficacy of silence. I visited a Trappist monastery in South Africa. A beautiful place it was. Most of the inmates of that place were under a vow of silence. I inquired of the Father the motive of it and he said the motive is apparent: 'We are frail human beings. We do not know very often what we say. If we want to listen to the still small Voice that is always speaking within us, it will not be heard if we continually speak.' I understood that precious lesson. I know the secret of silence.

Young India, 6-8-'25

Experience has taught me that silence is a part of the spiritual discipline of a votary of truth. Proneness to exaggerate, to suppress or modify the truth, wittingly or unwittingly, is a natural weakness of man, and silence is necessary in order to surmount it. A man of few words will rarely be thoughtless in his speech; he will measure every word. We find so many people impatient to talk. There is no chairman of a meeting who is not pestered with notes for permission to speak. And whenever the permission is given the speaker generally exceeds the time limit, asks for more time, and keeps on talking without permission. All this talking can hardly be said to be of any benefit to the world. It is so much waste of time.

Autobiography (1948), p.84

When one comes to think of it one cannot help feeling that nearly half the misery of the world would disappear if we, fretting mortals, knew the virtue of silence. Before modern civilization came upon us, at least six to eight hours of silence out of twenty-four were vouchsafed to us. Modern civilization has taught us to convert night into day and golden silence into brazen din and noise. What a great thing it would be if we in our busy lives could retire into ourselves each day for at least a couple of hours and prepare our minds to listen in. to the Voice of the Great Silence. The Divine Radio is always singing if we could only make ourselves ready to listen to it, but it is impossible to listen without silence. St. Theresa has used a charming image to sum up the sweet result of silence:

"You will at once feel your senses gather themselves together; they seem like bees which return to the hive and there shut themselves up to work without effort or care on your part. God thus rewards the violence which your soul has been doing to itself; and gives to it such a domination over the senses that a sign is enough when it desires to recollect itself, for them to obey and so gather themselves together. At the first call of the will they come back more and more quickly. At last after many and many exercises of this kind God disposes them to a state of absolute repose and of perfect contemplation."

Harijan, 24-9-'38

It (silence) has now become both a physical and spiritual necessity for me. Originally it was taken to relieve the sense of pressure. Then I wanted time for writing. After, however, I had practised it

for some time, I saw the spiritual value of it. It
suddenly flashed across my mind that that was the
time when I could best hold communion with God.
And now I feel as though I was naturally built for
silence.

Harijan, 10-12-'38

Silence is a great help to a seeker after truth
like myself. In the attitude of silence the soul finds
the path in a clearer light, and what is elusive and
deceptive resolves itself into crystal clearness. Our
life is a long and arduous quest after Truth, and
the soul requires inward restfulness to attain its
full height.

Harijan, 10-12-'38

19. EQUALITY OF RELIGIONS

Religions are different roads converging to the
same point. What does it matter that we take
different roads, so long as we reach the same goal?
In reality, there are as many religions as there are
individuals.

Hind Swaraj (1946), p.36

I believe that all the great religions of the world
are true more or less. I say 'more or less' because
I believe that every thing that the human hand
touches, by reason of the very fact that human
beings are imperfect, becomes imperfect. Perfection
is the exclusive attribute of God and it is
undescribable, untranslat-able. I do believe that it
is possible for every human being to become perfect
even as God is perfect. It is necessary for us all to
aspire after perfection, but when that blessed state
is attained, it becomes indescribable; indefinable.

And, I, therefore, admit, in all humility, that even the Vedas, the Koran and the Bible are imperfect word of God and, imperfect beings that we are, swayed to and fro by a multitude of passions, it is impossible for us even to understand this word of God in its fulness.

Young India, 22-9-'27

Belief in one God is the corner-stone of all religions. But I do not foresee a time when there would be only one religion on earth in practice. In theory, since there is one God, there can be only one religion. But in practice, no two persons I have known have had the same identical conception of God. Therefore, there will, perhaps, always be different religions answering to different temperaments and climatic conditions.

Harijan, 2-2-'34

The need of the moment is not one religion, but mutual respect and tolerance of the devotees of the different religions. We want to reach not the dead level, but unity in diversity. Any attempt to root out traditions, effects of heredity, climate and other surroundings is not only bound to fail but is a sacrilege. The soul of religions is one, but it is encased in a multitude of forms. The latter will persist to the end of time. Wise men will ignore the outward crust and see the same soul living under a variety of crusts.

Young India, 25-9-'25

There is in Hinduism room enough for Jesus, as there is for Mohammed, Zoroaster and Moses. For me the different religions are beautiful flowers from the same garden, or they are branches of the same majestic tree. Therefore they are equally true, though being received and interpreted through human instruments equally imperfect. It is impossible for me to reconcile myself to the idea of conversion after the style that goes on in India and elsewhere today. It is an error which is perhaps the greatest impediment to the world's progress towards peace. "Warring creeds" is a blasphemous expression. And it fitly describes the state of things in India, the mother, as I believe her to be, of Religion or religions. If she is truly the mother, the motherhood is on trial. Why should a Christian want to convert a Hindu to Christianity and vice versa ? Why should he not be satisfied if the Hindu is a good or godly man ? If the morals of a man are a matter of no concern, the form of worship in a particular manner in a church, a mosque or a temple is an empty formula; it may even be a hindrance to individual or social growth, and insistence on a particular form or repetition of a credo may be a potent cause of violent quarrels leading to bloodshed and ending in utter disbelief in Religion, i.e. God Himself.

Harijan, 30-1-'37

But it is no business of mine to criticize the scriptures of other faiths, or to point out their defects. It is and should be, however, my privilege to proclaim and practise the truths that there may be in them. I may not, therefore, criticize or condemn things in the Koran or the life of the Prophet that I cannot understand. But I welcome every opportunity to express my admiration for such aspects of his life as I have been able to appreciate and understand. As for things that present difficulties, I am content to see them through the eyes of devout Mussalman friends, while I try to understand them with the help of the writings of eminent Muslim expounders of Islam. It is only through such a reverential approach to faiths other than mine that I can realize the principle of equality of all religions. But it is both my right and duty to point out the defects in Hinduism in order to purify it and to keep it pure. But when non-Hindu critics set about criticizing Hinduism and cataloguing its faults they only blazon their own ignorance of Hinduism and their incapacity to regard it from the Hindu viewpoint. It destorts their vision and vitiates their judgment. Thus my own experience of the non-Hindu critics of Hinduism brings home to me my limitations and teaches me to be wary of launching on a criticism of Islam or Christianity and their founders.

Harijan, 13-3-'37

The Allah of Islam is the same as the God of Christians and the Ishwara of Hindus. Even as there are numerous names of God in Hinduism, there are as many names of God in Islam. The names do not indicate individuality but attributes, and little man has tried in his humble way to describe mighty God by giving Him attributes, though He is above all attributes, Indescribable, Inconceivable, Immeasurable. Living faith in this God means acceptance of the brotherhood of the mankind. It also means equal respect for all religions,

Harijan, 14-5-'38

20. TOLERANCE

I do not like the word tolerance, but could not think of a better one. Tolerance implies a gratuitous assumption of the inferiority of other faiths to one's own, whereas Ahimsa teaches us to entertain the same respect for the religious faiths of others as we accord to our own, thus admitting the imperfection of the latter. This admission will readily be made by a seeker of Truth who follows the law of love. If we had attained the full vision of Truth, we would no longer be seekers, but become one with God, for Truth is God. But being only seekers, we prosecute our quest and are conscious of our imperfection. And if we are imperfect ourselves, religion as conceived by us must also be imperfect. We have not realized religion in its perfection, even as we have not realized God. Religion of our conception, thus imperfect, is always subject to a process of evolution and re-interpretation. Progress towards Truth, towards God, is possible only because of such evolution. And if all faiths outlined by men are imperfect, the question of comparative merit does not arise. All faiths constitute a revelation of Truth, but all are imperfect and liable to error. Reverence to other faiths need not blind us to their faults. We must be keenly alive to the defects of our own faith, and must not leave it on that account but try to overcome those defects. Looking at all religions with an equal eye, we would not only not hesitate but would think it our duty to adopt into our faith every acceptable feature of other faiths.

The question then arises – Why should there be so many faiths? We know that there are a large variety of them. The soul is one, but the bodies which she animates are many. We cannot reduce the number of bodies; yet we recognize the unity of the soul. Even as a tree has a single trunk, but many branches and leaves, there is one Religion, but any number of faiths. All faiths are a gift of God, but partake of human imperfection, as they pass through the medium of humanity. God-given religion is beyond all speech. Imperfect men put it into such language as they can command, and their words are interpreted by other men equally imperfect. Whose interpretation must be held to be the right one ? Every one is right from his own standpoint, but it is not impossible that every one is wrong. Hence the necessity for tolerance, which does not mean indifference towards one's own faith, but a more intelligent and purer love for it. Tolerance gives us spiritual insight, which is as far from fanaticism as the north pole is from the south. True knowledge of religion breaks down the barriers between faith and faith and gives rise to tolerance. Cultivation of tolerance for other faiths will impart to us a truer understanding of our own.

Tolerance obviously does not disturb the distinction between right and wrong, or good and evil. The reference here throughout has been to the principal faiths of the world, which are all based on identical fundamental principles, and which can all point to saintly men and women who held them in the past and hold them now. In the case of good and evil, we have to cultivate charity for the wicked no less than for the good, the sinner no less than the saint, all the while we cherish inveterate hatred towards wickedness and sin.

Young India, (Bulletin), 2-10-'30

The golden rule of conduct, therefore, is mutual toleration, seeing that we will never all think alike and we shall see Truth in fragment and from different angles of vision. Conscience is not the same thing for all. Whilst, therefore, it is a good guide for individual conduct, imposition of that conduct upon all will be an insufferable interference with everybody's freedom of conscience.

Young India, 23-9-'26

21. CONVERSION
[From an address to foreign missionaries:]

You, the missionaries, come to India thinking that you come to a land of heathens, of idolaters, of men who do not know God. One of the greatest of Chrsitian Divines, Bishop Hebber, wrote the two lines which have always left the sting with me: 'Where every prospect pleases, and Man alone is vile'. I wish he had not written them. My own experience in my travels throughout India has been to the contrary. I have gone from one end of the country to the other, without any prejudice in a relentless search after truth, and I am not able to say that here in this fair land, watered by the great Ganga, the Brahmaputra and the Yamuna, man is vile. He is not vile. He is as much a seeker after truth as you and I are, possibly more so. This

reminds me of a French book translated for me by
a French friend. It is an account of an imaginary
expedition in search of knowledge. One party
landed in India and found Truth and God
personified, in a little Pariah's hut. I tell you there
are many such huts belonging to the untouchables
where you will certainly find God. They do not
reason but they persist in the belief that God is.
They depend upon God for His assistance and find
it too. There are many stories told throughout the
length and breadth of India about these noble
untouchables. Vile as some of them may be there
are noblest specimens of humanity in their midst.
But does my experience exhaust itself merely with
the untouchables? No. I am here to tell you that
there are non-Brahmanas, there are Brahmanas
who are as fine specimens of humanity as you will
find in any place on the earth. There are
Brahmanas today in India who are embodiments of
self-sacrifice, godliness and humility. There are
Brahmanas who are devoting themselves body and
soul to the service of untouchables, with no
expectation of reward from the untouchables, but
with execration from orthodoxy. They do not mind
it because in serving Pariahs they are serving God.
I can quote chapter and verse from my experience.
I place these facts before you in all humility for the
simple reason that you may know this land better,
the land to which you have come to serve. You are
here to find out the distress of the people of India
and remove it. But I hope you are here also in a
receptive mood and if there is anything that India
has to give, you will not stop your ears, you will
not close your eyes and steel your hearts but open
up your ears, eyes and most of all your hearts to

receive all that may be good in this land. I give
you my assurance that there is a great deal of good
in India. Do not flatter yourselves with the belief
that a mere recital of that celebrated verse in St.
John makes a man a Christian. If I have read the
Bible correctly, I know many men who have never
heard the name of Jesus Christ or have even
rejected the official interpretation of Christianity,
who will, probably, if Jesus came in our midst
today in the flesh, be owned by him more than
many of us. I therefore ask you to approach the
problem before you with open-heartedness and
humility.

I cannot help recalling to you the conversation I
related in Darjeeling at the Missionary language
School. Lord Salisbury was waited upon by a
deputation of missionaries in connection with
China and this deputation wanted protection. I
cannot recall the exact words but give you the
purport of the answer lord Salisbury gave. He said,
'Gentlemen, if you want to go to China to preach
the message of Christianity, then do not ask for
assistance of temporal power. Go with your lives in
your hands and if the people of China want to kill
you, imagine that you have been killed in the
service of God.' Lord Salisbury was right. Christian
missionaries come to India under the shadow, or, if
you like, under the protection of a temporal power,
and it creates an impassable bar.

If you give me statistics that so many orphans
have been reclaimed and brought to the Christian
faith, I would accept them but I do not feel
convinced thereby that it is your mission. In my
opinion your mission is infinitely superior to that.
You want to find men in India and if you want to

do that, you have to go to the lowly cottages not to give them something, might be to take something from them. A true friend as I claim to be of the missionaries of India and of the Europeans, I speak to you what I feel from the bottom of my heart. I miss receptiveness, humility, willingness on your part to identify yourselves with the masses of India. I have talked straight from my heart. May it find a response from your hearts.

Young India, 6-8-'25

I hold that proselytizing under the clock of humanitarian work is, to say the least, unhealthy. It is most certainly resented by the people here. Religion after all is a deeply personal matter, it touches the heart. Why should I change my religion because a doctor who professes Christianity as his religion has cured me of some disease or why should the doctor expect or suggest such a change whilst I am under his influence? Is not medical relief its own reward and satisfaction? Or why should I whilst I am in a missionary educational institution have Christian teaching thrust upon me? In my opinion these are not uplifting and give rise to suspicion if not even secret hostility. The methods of conversion must be like Caesar's wife above suspicion. Faith is not imparted like secular subjects. It is given through the language of the heart. If a man has a living faith in him, it spreads its aroma like the rose its scent. Because of its invisibility, the extent of its influence is far wider than that of the visible beauty of the colour of the petals.

I am, then, not against conversion. But I am against the modern methods of it. Conversion nowadays has become a matter of business, like any other. I remember having read a missionary report saying how much it cost per head to convert and then presenting a budget for 'the next harvest'.

Yes, I do maintain that India's great faiths are all-sufficing for her. Apart from Christianity and Judaism, Hinduism and its offshoots, Islam and Zoroastrianism are living faiths. No one faith is perfect. All faiths are equally dear to their respective votaries. What is wanted therefore is living friendly contact among the followers of the great religions of the world and not a clash among them in the fruitless attempt on the part of each community to show the superiority of its faith over the rest. Through such friendly contact it will be possible for us all to rid our respective faiths of shortcomings and excrescences.

It follows from what I have said above that India is in no need of conversion of the kind I have in mind. Conversion in the sense of self-purification, self-realization is the crying need of the times. That, however, is not what is ever meant by proselytizing. To those who would convert India, might it not be said, 'Physician, heal thyself'?

Young India, 23-4-'31

When I was a youth I remember a Hindu having become a convert to Christianity. The whole town understood that the initiation took the shape of this well-bread Hindu partaking of beef and brandy in the name of Jesus Christ and discarding his national costume. I learnt in later years, that such a convert, as so many of my missionary friends put it, came to a life of freedom out of a life of bondage, to a life of plenty out of one of penury. As I wander about throughout the length and breadth of India I see many Christian Indians almost ashamed of their birth, certainly of their ancestral religion, and of their ancestral dress. The aping of Europeans on the part of Anglo-Indians is bad enough,' but the aping of them by Indian converts is a violence done to their country and, shall I say, even to their new religion. There is a verse in the New Testament to bid Christians avoid meat if it would offend their neighbours. Meat here, I presume, includes drink and dress. I can appreciate uncompromising avoidance of all that is evil in the old, but where there is not only no question of anything evil but where an ancient practice may be even desirable, it would be a crime to part with it when one knows for certain that the giving up would deeply hurt relatives and friends. Conversion must not mean denationalization. Conversion should mean a definite giving up of the evil of the old, adoption of all the good of the new and a scrupulous avoidance of everything evil in the new. Conversion, therefore, should mean a life of greater dedication to one's own country, greater surrender to God, greater self-purification.... Is it not truly deplorable that many Christian Indians discard their own mother-tongue, bring up their children only to speak in English? Do they not thereby completely cut themselves adrift from the nation in whose midst they have to live?

Young India, 20-8-'25

To live the gospel is the most effective way... most effective in the beginning, in the middle and in the end. Preaching jars on me and makes no appeal to me, and I get suspicious of missionaries who preach. But I love those who never preach but live the life according to their lights. Their lives are silent, yet most effective testimonies. Therefore

I cannot say what to preach, but I can say that a life of service and uttermost simplicity is the best preaching. A rose does not need to preach. It simply spreads its fragrance. The fragrance is its own sermon. If it had human understanding and if it could engage a number of preachers, the preachers would not be able to sell more roses than the fragrance itself could do. The fragrance of religious and spiritual life is much finer and subtler than that of the rose.

Harijan, 29-3-'35

I could no more think of asking a Christian or a Mussalman or a Parsi or a Jew to change his faith than I would think of changing my own. This makes me no more oblivious of the limitations of the professors of those faiths, than it makes me of the grave limitations of the professors of mine. And seeing that it takes all my resources in trying to bring my practice to the level of my faith and in preaching the same to my co-religionists, I do not dream of preaching to the followers of other faiths. 'Judge not lest ye be judged' is a sound maxim for one's conduct. It is a conviction daily growing upon me that the great and rich Christian missions will render true service to India, if they can persuade themselves to confine their activities to humanitarian service without the ulterior motive of converting India or at least her unsophisticated villagers to Christianity, or destroying their social superstructure, which not withstanding its many defects has stood now from time immemorial the onslaughts upon it from within and from without. Whether they – the missionaries – and we wish it or not, what is true in the Hindu faith will abide, what is untrue will fall to pieces. Every living faith

must have within itself the power of rejuvenation if
it is to live.

Harijan, 28-9-'35

Shuddhi and Tabligh

In my opinion there is no such thing as
proselytism in Hinduism as it is understood in
Christianity or to a lesser extent in Islam. The
Arya Samaj has, I think, copied the Christians in
planning its propaganda. The modern method does
not appeal to me. It has done more harm than
good. Though regarded as a matter of the heart
purely and one between the Maker and oneself, it
has degenerated into an appeal to the selfish
instinct.... My Hindu instinct tells me that all
religions are more or less true. All proceed from
the same God but all are imperfect because they
have come down to us through imperfect human
instrumentality. The real Shuddhi movement
should consist in each one trying to arrive at
perfection in his or her own faith. In such a plan
character would be the only test. What is the use
of crossing from one compartment to another, if it
does not mean a moral rise? What is the meaning
of my trying to convert to the service of God (for
that must be the implication of Shuddhi or
Tabligh) when those who are in my fold are
everyday denying God by their actions? "Physician,
heal thyself" is more true in matters religious than
mundane.

Young India, 29-5-'24

22. WHY I AM A HINDU

Believing as I do in the influence of heredity, being born in a Hindu family, I have remained a Hindu. I should reject it, if I found it inconsistent with my moral sense or my spiritual growth. On examination I have found it to be the most tolerant of all religions known to me. Its freedom from dogma makes a forcible appeal to me inasmuch as it gives the votary the largest scope for self-expression. Not being an exlusive religion, it enables the followers of that faith not merely to respect all the other religions, but it also enables them to admire and assimilate whatever may be good in the other faiths. Non-violence is common to all religions, but it has found the highest expression and application in Hinduism. (I do not regard Jainism or Buddhism as separate from Hinduism.) Hinduism believes in the oneness not of merely all human life but in the oneness of all that lives. Its worship of the cow is, in my opinion, its unique contribution to the evolution of humanitarianism. It is a practical application of the belief in the oneness and, therefore, sacredness, of all life. The great belief in transmigration is a direct consequence of that belief. Finally the discovery of the law of Varnashrama is a magnificent result of the ceaseless search for truth.

Young India, 20-10-'27

I call myself a Sanatani Hindu, because,

73

(1) I believe in the Vedas, the Upanishads, the Puranas and all that goes by the name of Hindu scriptures, and therefore in Avataras and rebirth;

(2) I believe in the Varanshrama Dharma in a sense, in my opinion, strictly Vedic but not in its present popular and crude sense;

(3) I believe in the protection of the cow in its much larger sense than the popular;

(4) I do not disbelieve in idol-worship.

The reader will note that I have purposely refrained from using the word divine origin in reference to the Vedas or any other scriptures. For I do not believe in the exclusive divinity of the Vedas. I believe the Bible, the Koran, and the Zend Avesta to be as much divinely inspired as the Vedas. My belief in the Hindu scriptures does not require me to accept every word and every verse as divinely inspired. Nor do I claim to have any first-hand knowledge of these wonderful books. But I do claim to know and feel the truths of the essential teaching of the scriptures. I decline to be bound by any interpretation, however learned it may be, if it is repugnant to reason or moral sense. I do not emphatically repudiate the claim (if they advance any such) of the present Shankaracharyas and Shastris to give a correct interpretation of the Hindu scriptures. On the contrary I believe that our present knowledge of these books is in a most chaotic state. I believe implicitly in the Hindu aphorism, that no one truly knows the Shastras who has not attained perfection in Innocence (Ahimsa), Truth (Satya) and Self-control (Brahma-charya) and who has not renounced all acquisition or possession of wealth. I believe in the institution of Gurus, but in this age millions must go without

a Guru, because it is a rare thing to find a
combination of perfect purity and perfect learning.
But one need not despair of ever knowing the truth
of one's religion, because the fundamentals of
Hinduism, as of every great religion, are
unchangeable and easily understood. Every Hindu
believes in God and His oneness, in rebirth and
salvation.... I am a reformer through and through.
But my zeal never takes me to the rejection of any
of the essential things of Hinduism. I have said I
do not disbelieve in idol-worship. An idol does not
excite any feeling of veneration in me. But I think
that idol-worship is part of human nature. We
hanker after symbolism. Why should one be more
composed in a church than elsewhere? Images are
an aid to worship. No Hindu considers an image to
be God. I do not consider idol-worship a sin.

It is clear from the foregoing that Hinduism is
not an exclusive religion. In it there is room for the
worship of all the prophets of the world. It is not
a missionary religion in the ordinary sense of the
term. It has no doubt absorbed many tribes in its
fold, but this absorption has been of an
evolutionary, imperceptible character. Hinduism
tells everyone to worship God according to his own
faith or Dharma, and so it lives at peace with all
the religions.

Young India, 6-10-'21

23.
BUDDHISM, CHRISTIANITY AND ISLAM

I have heard it contended times without number and I have read in books also claiming to express the spirit of Buddhism that Buddha did not believe in God. In my humble opinion such a belief contradicts the very central fact of Buddha's teaching.... The confusion has arisen over his rejection and just rejection of all the base things that passed in his generation under the name of God. He undoubtedly rejected the notion that a being called God was actuated by malice, could repent of his actions, and like the kings of the earth could possibly be open to temptations and bribes and could possibly have favourites. His whole soul rose in mighty indignation against the belief that a being called God required for his satisfaction the living blood of animals in order that he might be pleased – animals who were his own creation. He, therefore, reinstated God in the right place and dethroned the usurper who for the time being seemed to occupy that White Throne. He emphasized and redeclared the eternal and unalterable existence of the moral government of this universe. He unhesitatingly said that the law was God Himself.

Young India, 24-11-'27

God's laws are eternal and unalterable and not separable from God Himself. It is an indispensable condition of His very perfection. And hence the great confusion that Buddha disbelieved in God and simply believed in the moral law, and because of this confusion about God Himself, arose the confusion about the proper understanding of the great word Nirvana. Nirvana is undoubtedly not utter extinction. So far as I have been able to understand the central fact of Buddha's life, Nirvana is utter extinction of all that is base in us, all that is vicious in us, all that is corrupt and curruptible in us. Nirvana is not like the black, dead peace of the grave, but the living peace, the living happiness of a soul which is conscious of itself, and conscious of having found its own abode in the heart of the Eternal.

Young India, 24-11-'27

Great as Buddha's contribution to humanity was in restoring God to His eternal place, in my humble opinion, greater still was his contribution to humanity in his exacting regard of all life, be it ever so low.

Young India, 20-1-'27

I may say that I have never been interested in a historical Jesus. I should not care if it was proved by someone that the man called Jesus never lived, and that (what) was narrated in the Gospels was a fragment of the writer's imagination. For the Sermon on the Mount would still be true for me.

Young India, 31-12-'31

I cannot ascribe exclusive divinity to Jesus. He is as divine as Krishna or Rama or Muhammad or Zoroaster. Similarly I do not regard every word of the Bible as the inspired word of God even as I do not regard every word of the Vedas or the Koran as inspired. The sum total of each of these books is certainly inspired, but I miss that inspiration in many of the things taken individually. The Bible is as much a book of religion with me as the Gita and the Koran.

Harijan, 6-3-'37

What... does Jesus mean to me? To me, He was one of the greatest teachers humanity has ever had. To His believers, He was God's only begotten Son. Could the fact that I do or do not accept this belief make Jesus have any more or less influence in my life? Is all the grandeur of His teaching and of His doctrine to be forbidden to me ? I cannot believe so.

The Modern Review, October, '41

I believe that it is impossible to estimate the merits of the various religions of the world, and, moreover, I believe that it is unnecessary and harmful even to attempt it. But each one of them, in my judgement, embodies a common motivating force : the desire to uplift man's life and give it purpose. And because the life of Jesus has the significance and the transcendency to which I have alluded, I believe that He belongs not solely to Christianity, but to the entire world, to all races and people-it matters little under what flag, name or doctrine they may work, profess a faith or worship a god inherited from their ancestors.

The Modem Review, October, '41

I have not been able to see any difference between the Sermon on the Mount and the Bhagavad Gita. What the Sermon describes in a graphic manner, the Bhagavad Gita reduces to a scientific formula. It may not be a scientific book in the accepted sense of the term, but it has argued out the law of love − the law of abandon as I

would call it – in a scientific manner. The Sermon
on the Mount gives the same law in wonderful
language. The New Testament gave me comfort
and boundless joy, as it came after the repulsion
that parts of the Old had given me. Today
supposing I was deprived of the Gita and forgot all
its contents but had a copy of the Sermon, I should
derive the same joy from it as I do from the Gita.

Young India, 22-12-'27

I do regard Islam to be a religion of peace in the
same sense as Christianity, Buddhism and
Hinduism are. No doubt there are differences in
degrees, but the object of these religions is peace.

Young India, 20-1-'27

Islam's distinctive contribution to India's national
culture is its unadulterated belief in the oneness of
God and a practical application of the truth of the
brotherhood of man for those who are nominally
within its fold. I call these two distinctive contribu-
tions. For in Hinduism the spirit of brotherhood
has become too much philosophized. Similarly
though philosophical Hinduism has no other god
but God, it cannot be denied that practical Hinduism is not so emphatically uncompromising as Islam.

Young India, 21-3-'29

24. GOD AND GODS

"If Hinduism become monotheistic," suggested
the Father, "Christianity and Hinduism can serve
India in co-operation."

"I would love to see the co-operation happen,"
said Gandhiji, "but it cannot if the present day
Christian Missions persist in holding up Hinduism

to ridicule and saying that no one can go to heaven unless he renounces and denounces Hinduism. But I can conceive a good Christian, silently working away, and shedding the sweet aroma of his life on Hindu communities, like the rose which does not need any speech to spread its fragrance but spreads it because it must. Even so a truly spiritual life. Then surely there would be peace on earth and goodwill among men. But not so long as there is militant or 'muscular' Christianity. This is not to be found in the Bible. But you find it in Germany and other countries."

"But if Indians begin to believe in one God and give up idolatry, don't you think the whole difficulty will be solved?"

"Will the Christians be satisfied with it? Are they all united?"

"Of course all the Christian sects are not united," said the Catholic Father.

"Then you are asking only a theoretical question. And may I ask you, is there any amalgamation between Islam and Christianity, though both are said to believe in one God? If these two have not amalgamated, there is less hope of amalgamation of Christians and Hindus along the lines you suggest. I have my own solution; but in the first instance, I dispute the description that Hindus believe in many gods and are idolaters. They do say there are many gods, but they also declare unmistakably that there is ONE GOD, the GOD of gods. It is, therefore, not proper to suggest that Hindus believe in many Gods. They certainly believe in many worlds. Just as there is a world inhabited by men, and another by beasts, so also is there one inhabited by superior beings called gods

whom we do not see but who nevertheless exist.
The whole mischief is created by the English
rendering of the word देव or देवता (Deva or Devata)
for which you have not found a better term than
'god'. But God is Ishwara, Devadhideva, God of
gods. So you see it is the word 'god' used to
describe different divine beings that has given rise
to such confusion. I believe that I am a thorough
Hindu but I never believe in many gods. Never
even in my childhood did I hold that belief, and no
one ever taught me to do so.

Idolatry

"As for idol-worship, you cannot do without it in
some form or other. Why does a Mussalman give
his life for defending a mosque which he calls a
house of God? And why does a Christian go to a
church, and when he is required to take an oath he
swears by the Bible? Not that I see any objection
to it. And what is it if not idolatry to give untold
riches for building mosques and tombs? And what
do the Roman Catholics do when they kneel before
Virgin Mary and before saints – quite imaginary
figures in stone or painted on canvas or glass?'"

"But," objected the Catholic Father, "I keep my
mother's photo and kiss it in veneration of her. But
I do not worship it, nor do I worship saints. When
I worship God, I acknowledge Him as Creator and
greater than any human being."

"Even so, it is not the stone we worship, but it
is God we worship in images of stone or metal
however rude they may be."

"But villagers worship stones as God."

"No, I tell you they do not worship anything that
is less than God. When you kneel before Virgin

Mary and ask for her intercession, what do you do? You ask to establish contact with God through her. Even so a Hindu seeks to establish contact with God through a stone image. I can understand your asking for the Virgin's intercession. Why are Mussalmans filled with awe and exultation when they enter a mosque ? Why, is not the whole universe a mosque ? And what about the magnificent canopy of heaven that spreads over you? Is it any less than a mosque? But I understand and sympathize with the Muslims. It is their way of approach to God. The Hindus have their own way of approach to the same Eternal Being. Our media of approach are different, but that does not make Him different."

"But the Catholics believe that God revealed to them the true way."

"But why do you say that the will of God is expressed only in one book called the Bible and not in others? Why do you circumscribe the power of God?"

"But Jesus proved that he had received the word of God through miracles."

"But that is Mohammed's claim too. If you accept Christian testimony you must accept Muslim testimony and Hindu testimony too."

"But Mohammed said he could not do miracles."

"No. He did not want to prove the existence of God by miracles. But he claimed to receive messages from God.'

Harijan, 13-3-'37

Incarnation

God is not a person. To affirm that He descends to earth every now and again in the form of a human being is a partial truth which merely signifies that such a person lives near to God. Inasmuch as God is omnipresent, He dwells within every human being and all may, therefore, be said to be incarnations of Him. But this leads us nowhere. Rama, Krishna, etc. are called incarnations of God because we attribute divine qualities to them. In truth they are creations of man's imagination. Whether they actually lived or not does not affect the picture of them in men's minds. The Rama and Krishna of history often present difficulties which have to be overcome by all manner of arguments.

The truth is that God is the force. He is the essence of life. He is pure and undefied consciousness. He is eternal. And yet, strangely enough, all are not able to derive either benefit from or shelter in the all-pervading living presence.

Electricity is a powerful force. Not all can benefit from it. It can only be produced by following certain laws. It is a lifeless force. Man can utilize it if he labours hard enough to acquire the knowledge of its laws.

The living force which we call God can similarly be found if we know and follow His law leading to the discovery of Him in us.

Harijan, 22-6-'47

Hindu Dharma is like a boundless ocean teeming with priceless gems. The deeper you dive, the more treasures you find. In Hindu religion, God is known by various names. Thousands of people look doubtless upon Rama and Krishna as historical figures and literally believe that God came down in person on earth in the form of Rama, the son of Dasharatha, and by worshipping him one can

attain salvation. The same thing holds good about
Krishna. History, imagination and truth have got
so inextricably mixed up. It is next to impossible to
disentangle them. I have accepted all the names
and forms attributed to God as symbols connoting
one formless omnipresent Rama. To me, therefore,
Rama described as the lord of Sita, son of
Dasharatha, is the all-powerful essence whose
name inscribed in the heart, removes all suffering-
mental, moral and physical.

Harijan, 2-6-'46

25. TEMPLES AND IDOLS

I do not regard the existence of a temple as a
sin or superstition. Some form of common worship,
and a common place of worship appear to be a
human necessity. Whether the temples should
contain images or not is a matter of temperament
and taste. I do not regard a Hindu or a Roman
Catholic place of worship containing images as
necessarily bad or superstitious, and a mosque or a
Protestant place of worship as good or free of
superstition merely because of their exclusion of
images. A symbol such as a Cross or a book may
easily become idolatrous, and therefore
superstitious. And the worship of the image of
Child Krishna or Virgin Mary may become
ennobling and free of all superstition. It depends
upon the attitude of the heart of the worshipper.

Young India, 5-11-'25

We the human family are not all philosophers.
We are of the earth very earthy, and we are not
satisfied with contemplating the Invisible God.

Somehow or other we want something which we can touch, something which we can see, something before which we can kneel down. It does not matter whether it is a book, or an empty stone building, or a stone building inhabited by numerous figures. A book will satisfy some, an empty building will satisfy some others, and many others will not be satisfied unless they see something inhabiting these empty buildings. Then I ask you to approach these temples not as if they represented a body of superstitions. If you will approach these temples with faith in them, you will know that each time you visit them you will come away from them purified and with your faith more and more in the living God.

Harijan, 23-1-'37

Temple-going is for the purification of the soul. The worshipper draws the best out of himself. In greeting a living being, he may draw the best out of the person greeted, if the greeting is selfless. A living being is more or less fallible like oneself. But in the temple, one worships the living God, perfect beyond imagination. Letters written to living persons often end in heart-breaking, even when they are answered, and there is no guarantee of their being always answered. Letters to God who, according to the devotee's imagination, resides in temples, require neither pen nor ink nor paper, not even speech. Mere mute worship constitutes the letter which brings its own unfailing answer. The whole function is a beautiful exercise of faith. Here there is no waste of effort, no heart-breaking, no danger of being misunderstood. The writer must try to understand the simple philosophy lying behind the worship in temples or mosques or churches. He will understand my meaning better if he will realize that I make no distinction between these different abodes of God. They are what faith has made them. They are an answer to man's craving somehow to reach the UNSEEN.

Harijan, 18-3-'33

I am both an idolater and an iconoclast in what I conceive to be the true senses of the terms. I value the spirit behind idol-worship. It plays a most important part in the uplift of the human race. And I would like to possess the ability to defend with my life the thousands of holy temples which sanctify this land of ours.

Young India, 28-8-'24

I am an iconoclast in the sense that I break down the subtle form of idolatry in the shape of fanaticism that refuses to see any virtue in any other form of worshipping the Deity save one's own. This form of idolatry is more deadly for being more fine and evasive than the tangible and gross form of worship that identifies the Deity with a little bit of a stone or a golden image.

Young India, 28-8-'24

Temples, churches and mosques very often show corruption, more often deterioration. Nevertheless, it would be impossible to prove that all priests are bad or have been bad and that all churches, temples and mosques are hotbeds of curruption and superstition. Nor does the arguement take note of this fundamental fact that no faith has done without a habitation; and I go further that in the very nature of things it cannot exist, so long as man remains as he is constituted. His very body has been rightly called the temple of the Holy Ghost, though innumerable such temples belie fact and are hot-beds of corruption used for dissoluteness. And I presume that it will be accepted as a conclusive answer to a sweeping suggestion that all bodies should be destroyed for the corruption of many, if it can be shown, as it can be, that there are some bodies which are proper temples of the Holy Ghost. The cause for the corruption of many bodies will have to be sought else-where. Temples of stone and mortar are nothing else than a natural extension of these human temples and though they were in their conception undoubtedly habitations of God like human temples, they have been subject to the same law of decay as the latter.

Harijan, 11-3-'33

I know of no religion or sect that has done or is doing without its House of God, variously described as a temple, a mosque, a church, a synagogue or an Agiari. Nor is it certain that any of the great reformers including Jesus destroyed or discarded temples altogether. All of them sought to banish corruption from temples as well as from society. Some of them, if not all, appear to have preached from temples. I have ceased to visit temples for years, but I do not regard myself on that account as a better person than before. My mother never missed going to the temple when she was in a fit state to go there. Probably her faith was far greater than mine, though I do not visit temples. There are millions whose faith is sustained through these temples, churches and mosques. They are not all blind followers of a superstition, nor are they fanatics. Superstition and fanaticism are not their monopoly. These vices have their root in our hearts and minds.

Harijan, 11-3-'33

26. TREE – WORSHIP

A correspondent writes:

"It is a common enough sight in this country to see men and women offering worship to stocks and stones and trees, but I was surprised to find, that even educated women belonging to the families of enthusiastic social workers were not above this practice. Some of these sisters and friends defend the practice by saying, that since it is founded on pure reverence for the divine in nature and no false beliefs, it cannot be classed as superstition, and they cite the names of Satyavan and Savitri whose memory, they say, they commemorate in that way. The argument does not convince me. May I request you to throw some light on the matter?"

I like this question. It raises the old, old question of image-worship. I am both a supporter and opponent of image-worship. When image-worship degenerates into idolatry and becomes encrusted with false beliefs and doctrines, it becomes a necessity to combat it as a gross social evil. On the other hand, image-worship in the sense of investing one's ideal with a concrete shape is inherent in man's nature, and even valuable as an aid to devotion. Thus we worship an image when we offer homage to a book which we regard as holy or sacred. We worship an image when we visit a temple or a mosque with a feeling of sanctity or reverence. Nor do I see any harm in all this. On the contrary, endowed as man is with a finite, limited understanding, he can hardly do otherwise. Even so far from seeing anything inherently evil or harmful in tree-worship, I find in it a thing instinct with a deep pathos and poetic beauty. It symbolizes true reverence for the entire vegetable kingdom, which with its endless panorama of beautiful shapes and forms, declares to us as it were with a million tongues the greatness and glory of God. Without vegetation our planet would not be able to support life even for a moment. In such a country especially, therefore, in which there is a scarcity of trees, tree-worship assumes a profound economic significance.

I therefore see no necessity for leading a crusade against tree-worship. It is true, that the poor simple-minded women who offer worship to trees have no reasoned understanding of the implications of their act. Possibly they would not be able to give any explanation as to why they perform it. They act in the purity and utter simplicity of their faith. Such faith is not a thing to be despised; it is a great and powerful force that we should treasure.

Far different, however, is the case of vows and prayers which votaries offer before trees. The offering of vows and prayers for selfish ends, whether offered in churches, mosques, temples or before trees and shrines, is a thing not to be encouraged. Making of selfish requests of offering of vows is not related to image-worship as effect and cause. A personal selfish prayer is bad whether made before an image or an unseen God.

Let no one, however, from this understand me to mean that I advocate tree-worship in general. I do not defend tree-worship because I consider it to be a necessary aid to devotion, but only because I recognize that God manifests Himself in innumerable forms in this universe, and every such manifestation commands my spontaneous reverence.

Young India, 26-9-'29

27. REASON AND FAITH

Experience has humbled me enough to let me realize the specific limitations of reason. Just as matter misplaced becomes dirt, reason misused becomes lunacy.

Young India, 14-10-'26

Rationalists are admirable beings, rationalism is a hideous monster when it claims for itself omnipotence. Attribution of omnipotence to reason is as bad a piece of idolatry as is worship of stock and stone believing it to be God. I plead not for the suppression of reason, but for a due recognition of that in us which sanctifies reason.

Young India, 19-10-'26

There are subjects where reason cannot take us far and we have to accept things on faith. Faith then does not contradict reason but transcends it. Faith is a kind of sixth sense which works in cases which are without the purview of reason.

Harijan, 6-3-'37

It is faith that steers us through stormy seas, faith that moves mountains and faith that jumps across the ocean. That faith is nothing but a living, wide-awake consciousness of God within. He who has achieved that faith wants nothing. Bodily diseased, he is spiritually healthy; physically poor, he rolls in spiritual riches.

Young India, 24-9-'25

Without faith this world would come to naught in a moment. True faith is appropriation of the reasoned experience of people whom we believe to have lived a life purified by prayer and penance. Belief, therefore, in prophets or incarnations who have lived in remote ages is not an idle superstition but a satisfaction of an inmost spiritual want.

Young India, 14-4-'27

Everyone has faith in God though everyone does not know it. For, everyone has faith in himself and that multiplied to the nth degree is God. The sum total of all that lives is God. We may not be God but we are of God – even as a little drop of water is of the ocean. Imagine it torn away from the ocean and flung millions of miles away. It becomes helpless torn from its surroundings and cannot feel the might and majesty of the ocean. But if some one could point out to it that it is of the ocean, its faith would revive, it would dance with joy and the whole of the might and majesty of the ocean would be reflected in it.

Harijan, 3-6-'39

Seeing God face to face is to feel that He is enthroned in our hearts even as a child feels a mother's affection without needing any demonstration. Does a child reason out the existence of a mother's love? Can he prove it to others? He triumphantly declares, 'It is.' So must it be with the existence of God. He defies reason. But He is experienced. Let us not reject the experience of Tulsidas, Chaitanya, Ramadas and a host of other spiritual teachers even as we do not reject that of mundane teachers.

Young India, 9-7-'25

28. SCRIPTURES

Mr Basil Mathews: Where do you find the seat of authority?

Gandhiji: It lies here (pointing to his breast). I exercise my judgment about every scripture, including the Gita. I cannot let a scriptural text supersede my reason. Whilst I believe that the principal books are inspired, they suffer from a process of double distillation. Firstly they come through a human prophet, and then through the commentaries of interpreters. Nothing in them comes from God directly. Mathew may give one version of one text and John may give another. I cannot surrender my reason whilst I subscribe to divine revelation. And above all, 'the letter killeth, the spirit giveth life.' But you must not misunderstand my position. I believe in faith also, in things where reason has no place, e.g. the existence of God. No argument can move me from that faith, and like that little girl who repeated against all reason 'yet we are seven' I would like to repeat, on being baffled in argument by a very superior intellect, 'Yet there is God'.

Harijan, 5-12-'36

Divine knowledge is not borrowed from books. It has to be realized in oneself. Books are at best an aid, often even a hindrance.

Young India, 17-7-'24

An error does not become truth by reason of multiplied propagation, nor does truth become error because nobody sees it.

Young India, 26-2-'25

I would reject all authority if it is in conflict with sober reason or the dictates of the heart. Authority sustains and ennobles the weak when it is the handiwork of reason, but it degrades them when it supplants reason, sanctioned by the still small Voice within.

Young India, 8-12-'20

I am not a literalist. Therefore I try to understand the spirit of the various scriptures of the world. I apply the test of Truth and Ahimsa laid down by these very scriptures for interpretation. I reject what is inconsistent with that test, and I appropriate all that is consistent with it. The story of a Shudra having been punished by Ramachandra for daring to learn the Vedas I reject as an interpolation. And in any event, I worship Rama, the perfect being of my conception, not a historical person facts about whose life may vary with the progress of new historical discoveries and researches. Tulsidas had nothing to do with the Rama of history. Judged by historical test, his Ramayana would be fit for the scrap-heap. As a spiritual experience, his book is almost unrivalled at least for me. And then, too, I do not swear by every word that is to be found in so many editions published as the Ramayana of Tulsidas. It is the spirit running through the book that holds me spell-bound.

Young India, 27-8-'25

I have no knowledge that the Krishna of Mahabharata ever lived. My Krishna has nothing to do with any historical person. I would refuse to bow my head to the Krishna who would kill because his pride is hurt, or the Krishna whom the non-Hindus portray as a dissolute youth. I believe in Krishna of my imagination as a perfect incarnation, spotless in every sense of the word, the inspirer of the Gita and the inspirer of the lives of millions of human beings. But if it was proved to me that the Mahabharata is history in the sense that modern historical books are, that every word of the Mahabharata is authentic and the Krishna of the Mahabharata actually did some of the acts attributed to him, even at the risk of being banished from the Hindu fold I should not hesitate to reject that Krishna as God incarnate. But to me the Mahabharata is a profoundly religious book, largely allegorical, in no way meant to be a historical record. It is the description of the eternal duel going on within ourselves, given so vividly as to make us think for the time being that the deeds described therein were actually done by the human beings. Nor do I regard the Mahabharata as we have it now as a faultless copy of the original. On the contrary I consider that it has undergone many amendations.

Young India, 1-10-'25

A prayerful study and experience are essential for a correct interpretation of the scriptures. The injunction that a Shudra may not study the scriptures is not entirely without meaning. A Shudra means a spiritually uncultured, ignorant man. He is more likely than not to misinterpret the Vedas and other scriptures. Everyone cannot solve an algebraical equation. Some preliminary study is a *sine qua non.* How ill the grand truth 'I am

Brahman' lie in the mouth of a man steeped in sin!
To what ignoble purposes would he turn it! What
a distortion it would suffer at his hands!

A man, therefore, who would interpret the
scriptures must have the spiritual discipline. He
must practise the Yamas and Niyamas – the
eternal guides of conduct. A superficial practice
thereof is useless. The Shastras have enjoined the
necessity of a Guru. But a Guru being rare in
these days, a study of modern books inculcating
bhakti has been suggested by the sages. Those who
are lacking in *bhakti*, lacking in faith, are ill
qualified to interpret the scriptures. The learned
may draw an elaborately learned inter-pretation
out of them, but that will not be the true
interpretation. Only the experienced will arrive at
the true interpretation of the scriptures.

But even for the inexperienced there are certain
canons. That interpretation is not true which
conflicts with Truth. To one who doubts even
Truth, the scriptures have no meaning. No one can
contend with him.

Young India, 12-11-'25

29. THE MESSAGE OF THE GITA

1. Even in 1888-89, when I first became
acquainted with the Gita, I felt that it was not a
historical work, but that under the guise of
physical warfare, it described the duel that
perpetually went on in the hearts of mankind, and
that physical warfare was brought in merely to
make the description of the internal duel more
alluring. This preliminary intuition became more

confirmed on a closer study of religion and the Gita. A study of the Mahabharata gave it added confirmation. I do not regard the Mahabharata as a historical work in the accepted sense. The Adiparva contains powerful evidence in support of my opinion. By ascribing to the chief actors superhuman or subhuman origins, the great Vyasa made short work of the history of kings and their peoples. The persons therein described may be historical, but the author of the Mahabharata has used them merely to drive home his religious theme.

2. The author of the Mahabharata has not established the necessity of physical warfare; on the contrary he has proved its futility. He has made the victors shed tears of sorrow and repentance, and has left them nothing but a legacy of miseries.

3. In this great work the Gita is the crown. Its second chapter, instead of teaching the rules of physical warfare, tells us how a perfected man is to be known. In the characteristics of the perfected man of the Gita, I do not see any to correspond to physical warfare. Its whole design is inconsistent with the rules of conduct governing the relations between warring parties.

4. Krishna of the Gita is perfection and right knowledge personified; but the picture is imaginary. That does not mean that Krishna, the adored of his people, never lived. But perfection is imagined. The idea of a perfect incarnation is an aftergrowth.

5. In Hinduism, incarnation is ascribed to one who has performed some extraordinary service of mankind. All embodied life is in reality an incarnation of God, but it is not usual to consider

every living being an incarnation. Future generations pay this homage to one who, in his own generation, has been extraordinarily religious in his conduct. I can see nothing wrong in this procedure; it takes nothing from God's greatness, and there is no violence done to Truth. There is an Urdu saying which means, "Adam is not God but he is a spark of the Divine." And therefore he who is the most religiously behaved has most of the divine spark in him. It is in accordance with this train of thought that Krishna enjoys, in Hinduism, the status of the most perfect incarnation.

6. This belief in incarnation is a testimony of man's lofty spiritual ambition. Man is not at peace with himself till he has become like unto God. The endeavour to reach this state is the supreme, the only ambition worth having. And this is self-realization. This self-realization is the subject of the Gita, as it is of all scriptures. But its author surely did not write it to establish that doctrine. The object of the Gita appears to me to be that of showing the most excellent way to attain self-realization. That which is to be found, more or less clearly, spread out here and there in Hindu religious books, has been brought out in the clearest possible language in the Gita even at the risk of repetition.

7. *That matchless remedy is renunciation of the fruits of action.*

8. This is the centre round which the Gita is woven. This renunciation is the central sun, round which devotion, knowledge and the rest revolve like planets. The body has been likened to a prison. There must be action where there is body. Not one embodied being is exempted from labour. And yet

all religions proclaim that it is possible for man, by treating the body as the temple of God, to attain freedom. Every action is tainted, be it ever so trivial. How can the body be made the temple of God ? In other words how can one be free from action, i.e. from the taint of sin? The Gita has answered the question in decisive language: "By desireless action; by renouncing the fruits of action; by dedicating all activities to God, i.e. by surrendering oneself to Him body and soul."

9. But desirelessness or renunciation does not come for the mere talking about it. It is not attained by an intellectual feat. It is attainable only by a constant heart-churn. Right knowledge is necessary for attaining renunciation. Learned men possess a knowledge of a kind. They may recite the Vedas from memory, yet they may be steeped in self-indulgence. In order that knowledge may not run riot, the author of the Gita has insisted on devotion accompanying it and has given it the first place. Knowledge without devotion will be like a misfire. Therefore, says the Gita, "Have devotion, and knowledge will follow." This devotion is not mere lip-worship, it is a wrestling with death. Hence the Gita's assessment of the devotee's qualities is similar to that of the sage's.

10. Thus the devotion required by the Gita is no soft-hearted effusiveness. It certainly is not blind faith. The devotion of the Gita has the least to do with externals. A devotee may use, if he likes, rosaries, forehead marks, make offerings, but these things are no test of his devotion. He is the devotee who is jealous of none, who is a fount of mercy, who is without egotism, who is selfless, who treats alike cold and heat, happiness and misery, who is

ever forgiving, who is always contented, whose resolutions are firm, who has dedicated mind and soul to God, who causes no dread, who is not afraid of others, who is free from exultation, sorrow and fear, who is pure, who is versed in action and yet remains unaffected by it, who renounces all fruit, good or bad, who treats friend and foe alike, who is untouched by respect or disrespect, who is not puffed up by praise, who does not go under when people speak ill of him, who loves silence and solitude, who has a disciplined reason. Such devotion is inconsistent with the existence at the same time of strong attachments.

11. We thus see, that to be a real devotee is to realize oneself. Self-realization is not something apart. One rupee can purchase for us poison or nectar, but knowledge or devotion cannot buy us either salvation or bondage. These are not media of exchange. They are themselves the thing we want. In other words if the means and the end are not identical, they are almost so. The extreme of means is salvation. Salvation of the Gita is perfect peace.

12. But such knowledge and devotion, to be true, have to stand the test of renunciation of fruits of action. Mere knowledge of right and wrong will not make one fit for salvation. According to common notions, a mere learned man will pass as a Pandit. He need not perform any service. He will regard it as bondage even to lift a little *lota*. Where one test of knowledge is non-liability for service, there is no room for such mundane work as the lifting of a *lota*.

13. Or take *bhakti*. The popular notion of *bhakti* is soft-heartedness, telling beads and the like and disdaining to do even a loving service, lest the

telling of beads etc. might be interrupted. This
bhakta therefore leaves the rosary only for eating,
drinking and the like, never for grinding corn or
nursing patients.

14. But the Gita says: "No one has attained his
goal without action. Even men like Janaka attained
salvation through action. If even I were lazily to
cease working, the world would perish. How much
more necessary then for the people at large to
engage in action?"

15. While on the one hand it is beyond dispute
that all action binds, on the other hand it is
equally true that all living beings have to do some
work whether they will or no. Here all activity,
whether mental or physical, is to be included in
the term action. Then how is one to be free from
the bondage of action, even though he may be
acting? The manner in which the Gita has solved
the problem is, to my knowledge, unique. The Gita
says: "Do your allotted work but renounce its fruit-
be detached and work – have no desire for reward
and work."

This is the unmistakable teaching of the Gita.
He who gives up action falls. He who gives up only
the reward rises. But renunciation of fruit in no
way means indifference to the result. In regard to
every action one must know the result that is
expected to follow, the means thereto, and the
capacity for it. He, who, being thus equipped, is
without desire for the result, and is yet wholly
engrossed in the due fulfilment of the task before
him, is said to have renounced the fruits of his
action.

16. Again, let no one consider renunciation to
mean want of fruit for the renouncer. The Gita

reading does not warrant such a meaning. Renunciation means absence of hankering after fruit. As a matter of fact, he who renounces reaps a thousandfold. The renunciation of the Gita is the acid test of faith. He who is ever brooding over result often loses nerve in the performance of his duty. He becomes impatient and then gives vent to anger and begins to do unworthy things; he jumps from action to action, never remaining faithful to any. He who broods over results is like a man given to objects of senses; he is ever distracted, he says goodbye to all scruples, everything is right in his estimation and he therefore resorts to means fair and foul to attain his end.

17. From the bitter experiences of desire for fruit the author of the Gita discovered the path of renunciation of fruit, and put it before the world in a most convincing manner. The common belief is that religion is always opposed to material good. "One cannot act religiously in mercantile and such other matters. There is no place for religion in such pursuits; religion is only for attainment of salvation," we hear many worldly-wise people say. In my opinion the author of the Gita has dispelled this delusion. He has drawn no line of demarcation between salvation and wordly pursuits. On the contrary, he has shown that religion must rule even our wordly pursuits. I have felt that the Gita teaches us that what cannot be followed out in day-to-day practice cannot be called religion. Thus, according to the Gita, all acts that are incapable of being performed without attachment are taboo. This golden rule saves mankind from many a pitfall. According to this interpretation murder, lying, dissoluteness and the like must be regarded

as sinful and therefore taboo. Man's life then becomes simple, and from that simpleness springs peace.

18. Thinking along these lines, I have felt that in trying to enforce in one's life the central teaching of the Gita, one is bound to follow truth and Ahimsa. When there is no desire for fruit, there is no temptation for untruth or Himsa. Take any instance of untruth or violence, and it will be found that at its back was the desire to attain the cherished end. But it may be freely admitted that the Gita was not written to establish Ahimsa. It was an accepted and primary duty even before the Gita age. The Gita had to deliver the message of renunciation of fruit. This is clearly brought out so early as the second chapter.

19. But if the Gita believed in Ahimsa or it was included in desirelessness, why did the author take a warlike illustration? When the Gita was written, although people believed in Ahimsa, wars were not only not taboo but nobody observed the contradiction between them and Ahimsa.

20. In assessing the implications of renunciation of fruit, we are not required to probe the mind of the author of the Gita as to his limitations of Ahimsa and the like. Because a poet puts a particular truth before the world, it does not necessarily follow that he has known or worked out all its great consequences, or that having done so, he is able always to express them fully. In this perhaps lies the greatness of the poem and the poet. A poet's meaning is limitless. like man, the meaning of great writings suffers evolution. On examining the history of languages, we notice that the meaning of important words has changed or expanded. This is true of the Gita. The author has

himself extended the meanings of some of the current words. We are able to discover this even on a superficial examination. It is possible, that in the age prior to that of the Gita, offering of animals in sacrifice was permissible. But there is not a trace of it in the sacrifice in the Gita sense. In the Gita continuous concentration on God is the king of sacrifices. The third chapter seems to show that sacrifice chiefly means body-labour for service. The third and the fourth chapters read together will give us other meanings for sacrifice but never animal-sacrifice. Similarly has the meaning of the word Sannyasa undergone, in the Gita, a transformation. The Sannyasa of the Gita will not tolerate complete cessation of all activity. The Sannyasa of the Gita is all work and yet no work. Thus the author of the Gita by extending meanings of words has taught us to imitate him. Let it be granted, that according to the letter of the Gita it is possible to say that warfare is consistent with renunciation of fruit. But after 40 years' unremitting endeavour fully to enforce the teaching of the Gita in my own life, I have, in all humility, felt that perfect renunciation is impossible without perfect observance of Ahimsa in every shape and form.

21. The Gita is not an aphoristic work; it is a great religious poem. The deeper you dive into it, the richer the meanings you get. It being meant for the people at large, there is pleasing repetition. With every age the important words will carry new and expanding meanings. But its central teaching will never vary. The seeker is at liberty to extract from this treasure any meaning he likes so as to enable him to enforce in his life the central teaching.

22. Nor is the Gita a collection of Do's and Don'ts. What is lawful for one may be unlawful for another. What may be permissible at one time, or in one place, may not be so at another time, and in another place. Desire for fruit is the only universal prohibition. Desirelessness is obligatory.

23. The Gita has sung the praises of knowledge, but it is beyond the mere intellect; it is essentially addressed to the heart and capable of being understood by the heart. Therefore the Gita is not for those who have no faith. The author makes Krishna say:

"Do not entrust this treasure to him who is without sacrifice, without devotion, without the desire for this teaching and who denies Me. On the other hand those who will give this precious treasure to my devotees will by the fact of this service assuredly reach Me. And those who, being free from malice will with faith absorb this teaching, shall, having attained freedom, live where people of true merit go after death."
Young India, 6-8-'31

30. BEAUTY IN TRUTH

There are two aspects of thing-the outward and the inward. It is purely a matter of emphasis with me. The outward has no meaning except in so far as it helps the inward. All true art is thus the expression of the soul. The outward forms have value only in so far as they are the expression of the inner spirit in man. Art of that nature has the greatest possible appeal for me. But I know that many call themselves artists, and are recognized as such, and yet in their works there is absolutely no trace of the soul's upward urge and unrest.

All true art must help the soul to realize its inner self. In my own case, I find that I can do entirely without external forms in my soul's realization. I can claim, therefore, that there is truly efficient art in my life, though you might not see what you call works of art about me. My room may have blank walls; and I may even dispense with the roof, so that I may gaze out at the starry heavens overhead that stretch in an unending expanse of beauty. What conscious art of man can give me the panoramic scenes that open out before me, when I look up to the sky above with all its shining stars? This, however, does not mean that I refuse to accept the value of production of arts, generally accepted as such, but only that I personally feel how inadequate these are compared with the eternal symbols of beauty in Nature. These productions of man's art have their value only in so far as they help the soul onward towards self-realization.

I see and find beauty in Truth or through Truth. All Truths, not merely true ideas, but truthful faces, truthful pictures, or songs are highly beautiful. People generally fail to see Beauty in Truth, the ordinary man runs away from and becomes blind to the beauty in it. Whenever men begin to see Beauty in Truth, then true art will arise.

To a true artist only that face is beautiful which, quite apart from its exterior, shines with the Truth within the soul. There is... no Beauty apart from Truth. On the other hand, Truth may manifest itself in forms which may not be outwardly

T.G.-8

beautiful at all. Socrates, we are told, was the most truthful man of his time, and yet his features are said to have been the ugliest in Greece. To my mind he was beautiful because all his life was a striving after Truth, and you may remember that this outward form did not prevent Phidias from appreciating the beauty of Truth in him, though as an artist he was accustomed to see Beauty in outward forms also.

Truth and untruth often co-exist; good and evil are often found together. In an artist also, not seldom, the right perception of things and the wrong co-exist. Truly beautiful creations come when right perception is at work. If these moments are rare in life they are also rare in art.

These beauties ('a sunset or a crescent moon that shines amid the stars at night') are truthful, inasmuch as they make me think of the Creator at the back of them. How else could these be beautiful, but for the Truth that is in the centre of creation? When I admire the wonder of a sunset or the beauty of the moon, my soul expands in worship of the Creator. I try to see Him and His mercies in all these creations. But even the sunsets and sunrises would be mere hindrances if they did not help me to think of Him. Anything, which is a hindrance to the flight of the soul, is a delusion and a snare; even like the body, which often does actually hinder you in the path of salvation.

Young India, 13-11-'24

Truth is the first thing to be sought for, and Beauty and Goodness will then be added unto you. That is what Christ really taught in the Sermon on the Mount. Jesus was, to my mind, a supreme artist because he saw and expressed Truth; and so

was Muhammad, the Koran being the most perfect
composition in all Arabic literature--at any rate,
that is what scholars say. It is because both of
them strove first for Truth that the grace of
expression naturally came in and yet neither Jesus
nor Muhammad wrote on art. That is the Truth
and Beauty I crave for, live for, and would die for.

Young India, 20-11-'24

Here too, just as elsewhere, I must think in
terms of the millions. And to the millions we
cannot give that training to acquire a perception of
Beauty in such a way as to see Truth in it. Show
them Truth first and they will see Beauty
afterwards.... Whatever can be useful to... starving
millions is beautiful to my mind. Let us give today
first the vital things of life and all the graces and
ornaments of life will follow.

Young India, 20-11-'24

True art takes note not merely of form but also
of what lies behind. There is an art that kills and
an art that gives life. True art must be evidence of
happiness, contentment and purity of its authors.

Young India, 11-8-'21

We have somehow accustomed ourselves to the
belief that art is independent of the purity of
private life. I can say with all the experience at my
command that nothing could be more untrue. As I
am nearing the end of my earthly life I can say
that purity of life is the highest and truest art. The
art of producing good music from a cultivated voice
can be achieved by many, but the art of producing
that music from the harmony of a pure life is
achieved very rarely.

Harijan, 19-2-'38

31. RAMANAMA

Though my reason and heart long ago realized the highest attribute and name of God as Truth, I recognize truth by the name of Rama. In the darkest hour of my trial, that one name has saved me and is still saving me. It may be the association of childhood, it may be the fascination that Tulsidas has wrought on me. But the potent fact is there, and as I write these lines, my memory revives the scenes of my childhood when I used daily to visit the Ramji Mandir adjacent to my ancestral home. My Rama then resided there. He saved me from many fears and sins. It was no superstition for me. The custodian of the idol may have been a bad man. I know nothing against him. Misdeeds might have gone on in the temple. Again I know nothing of them. Therefore, they would not affect me. What was and is true of me is true of millions of Hindus.

Harijan, 18-3-'33

I laugh within myself when someone objects that Rama or the chanting of Ramanama is for the Hindus only, how can Mussulmans therefore take part in it? Is there one God for the Mussulmans and another for the Hindus, Parsis, or Christians ? No, there is only one omnipotent and omnipresent God. He is named variously and we remember Him by the name which is most familiar to us.

My Rama, the Rama of our prayers is not the

historical Rama, the son of Dasharatha, the King of
Ayodhya. He is the eternal, the unborn, the one
without a second. Him alone I worship. His aid
alone I seek, and so should you. He belongs equally
to all. I, therefore, see no reason why a Mussulman
or anybody should object to taking His name. But
he is in no way bound to recognize God as
Ramanama. He may utter to himself Allah or
Khuda so as not to mar the harmony of the sound.

Harijan, 28-4-'46

I myself have been a devotee of Tulsidas from
my childhood and have, therefore, always
worshipped God as Rama. But I know that if,
beginning with Omkar, one goes through the entire
gamut of God's names current in all climes, all
countries and languages, the result is the same. He
and His Law are one. To observe His Law is,
therefore, the best form of worship. A man who
becomes one with the Law does not stand in need
of vocal recitation of the name. In other words, an
individual with whom contemplation on God has
become as natural as breathing is so filled with
God's spirit that knowledge or observance of the
Law becomes second nature, as it were, with him.
Such a one needs no other treatment.

The question then arises as to why, in spite of
having this prince of remedies at hand, we know so
little about it and why even those who know, do
not remember Him or remember Him only by lip-
service, not from the heart. Parrot-like repetition of
God's name signifies failure to recognize Him as
the panacea for all ills.

Harijan, 24-3-'46

A devotee of Rama may be said to be the same
as the steadfast one (Sthitaprajnya) of the Gita. If

one goes a little deeper it will be seen that a true
devotee of God faithfully obeys the five elemental
forces of Nature. If he so obeys, he will not fall ill.
If perchance he does, he will cure himself with the
aid of the elementals. It is not for the dweller in
the body to get the body cured anyhow-he who
believes that he is nothing but body will naturally
wander to the ends of the earth in order to cure
the body of its ills. But he who realizes that the
soul is something apart from, though in the body
that it is imperishable in contrast to the perishable
body, will not be perturbed nor mourn if the
elementals fail. On the contrary he will welcome
death as a friend. He will become his own healer
instead of seeking for medical men. He will live in
the consciousness of the soul within and look to the
care, first and last, of the in-dweller.

Such a man will take God's name with every
breath. His Rama will be awake even whilst the
body is asleep. Rama will always be with him in
whatever he does. The real death for such a
devoted man will be the loss of this sacred
companionship.

As an aid to keeping his Rama with him, he will
take what the five elementals have to give him.
That is to say he will employ the simplest and
easiest way of deriving all the benefit he can from
earth, air, water, sunlight and ether. This aid is
not complementary to Ramanama. It is but a
means of its realization. Ramanama does not in
fact require any aid. But to claim belief in
Ramanama and at the same time to run to doctors
do not go hand in hand.

Just as the body cannot exist without blood, so
the soul needs the matchless and pure strength of

faith. This strength can renovate the weakness of all man's physical organs That is why it is said that when Ramanama is enshrined in the heart, it means the rebirth of man. This law applies to the young, the old, man and woman alike.

Harijan, 29-6-'47

32. NATURE CURE

Nature Cure treatment means that treatment which befits man. By "man" is meant not merely man as animal, but as creature possessing, in addition to his body, both mind and soul. For such a being Ramanama is the truest Nature Cure treatment. It is an unfailing remedy. The expression Ramabana or infallible cure is derived from it. Nature, too, indicates that for man it is the worthy remedy. No matter what the ailment from which a man may be suffering, recitation of Ramanama from the heart is the sure cure. God has many names. Each person can choose the name that appeals most to him. Ishwara, Allah, Khuda, God mean the same. But the recitation must not be parrotlike, it must be born of faith of which endeavour will be some evidence. What should the endeavour consist of ? Man should seek out and be content to confine the means of cure to the five elements of which the body is composed, i.e. earth, water, *akash,* sun and air. Of course, Ramanama must be the invariable accompaniment. If in spite of this, death supervenes, we may not mind. On the contrary, it should be welcomed. Science has not so far discovered any recipe for making the body immortal. Immortality is an attribute of the

soul. That is certainly imperishable, but it is man's
duty to try to express its purity.

Harijan, 3-3-'46

If we accept the above reasoning, it will
automatically limit the means permissible under
Nature Cure. And man is thereby saved from all
the paraphernalia of big hospitals and eminent
doctors etc. The large majority of persons in the
world can never afford these. Why, then, should
the few desire what the many cannot have?

Harijan, 3-3-'46

The potency of Ramanama is, however, subject to
certain conditions and limitations. Ramanama is
not like black magic. If someone suffers from
surfeit and wants to be cured of its after-effects so
that he can again indulge himself at the table,
Ramanama is not for him. Ramanama can be used
only for a good, not for an evil end, or else thieves
and robbers would be the greatest devotees.
Ramanama is for the pure in heart and for those
who want to attain purity and remain pure. It can
never be a means for self-indulgence. The remedy
for surfeit is fasting, not prayer. Prayer can come
in only when fasting has done its work. It can
make fasting easy and bearable. Similarly, the
taking of Ramanama will be a meaningless force
when at the same time you are drugging your
system with medicines. A doctor who uses his
talent to pander to the vices of his patient
degrades himself and his patient. What worse
degradation can there be for man than that instead
of regarding his body as an instrument of
worshipping his Maker, he should make it the
object of adoration and waste money like water to
keep it going anyhow? Ramanama, on the other

hand, purifies while it cures, and, therefore, it elevates. Therein lies its use as well as its limitation.

Harijan, 7-4-'46

An apt question is as to why a man who recites Ramanama regularly and leads a pure life should ever fall ill. Man is by nature imperfect. A thoughtful man strives after perfection, but never attains it. He stumbles on the way, however, unwittingly. The whole of God's law is embodied in a pure life. The first thing is to realize one's limitations. It should be obvious that the moment one transgresses those limits one falls ill. Thus a balanced diet eaten in accordance with needs gives one freedom from disease. How is one to know what is the proper diet for one? Many such enigmas can be imagined. The purport of it all is that every one should be his own doctor and find out his limitations. The man who does so will surely live up to 125.

Harijan, 19-5-'46

My love of Nature Cure and of indigenous systems does not blind me to the advance that Western medicine has made in spite of the fact that I have stigmatized it as black magic. I have used the harsh term and I do not withdraw it, because of the fact, that it has countenanced vivisection and all the awfulness it means and because it will stop at no practice, however bad it may be, if it prolongs the life of the body and because it ignores the immortal soul which resides in the body. I cling to Nature Cure in spite of its great limitations and in spite of the lazy pretensions of Nature curists. Above all, in Nature Cure, everybody can be his or her own doctor, not so in the various systems of medicine.

Harijan, 11-8-'46

Spiritual force is like any other force at the service of man. Apart from the fact that it has been used for physical ailments for ages, with more or less success, it would be intrinsically wrong not to use it, if it can be successfully used for the cure of physical ailments. For, man is both matter and spirit, each acting on and affecting the other. If you get rid of malaria by taking quinine, without thinking of the millions who do not get it, why should you refuse to use the remedy which is within you, because millions will not use it through their ignorance? May you not be clean and well because millions of others will not be so, ignorantly or, may be, even cussedly? If you will not be clean out of false notions of philanthropy, you will deny yourselves the duty of serving the very millions by remaining dirty and ill. Surely refusal to be spiritually well or clean is worse than the refusal to be physically clean and well.

Harijan, 1-9-'46

Salvation is nothing more and nothing less than being well in every way. Why should you deny it for yourselves, if thereby you show the way to others and beyond showing it, actually serve them in addition by reason of your fitness?

Harijan, 1-9-'46

33. UNITY OF ALL LIFE

My ethics not only permit me to claim but require me to own kinship with not merely the ape but the horse and the sheep, the lion and the leopard, the snake and the scorpion. (Not so need these kinsfolk regard themselves.) The hard ethics which rule my life, and I hold ought to rule that of every man and woman, imposes this unilateral obligation upon us. And it is so imposed because man alone is made in the image of God. That some of us do not recognize that status of ours, makes no difference, except that then we do not get the benefit of the status, even as a lion brought up in the company of sheep may not know his own status and, therefore, does not receive its benefits; but it belongs to him nevertheless, and, the moment he realizes it, he begins to exercise his dominion over the sheep. But no sheep masquerading as a lion can ever attain the leonine status. And, to prove the proposition, that man is made in the image of God, it is surely unnecessary to show that all men admittedly exhibit that image in their own persons. It is enough to show that one man at least has done so. And, will it be denied that the great religious teachers of mankind have exhibited the image of God in their own persons?

Young India, 8-7-'26

I do not want to live at the cost of the life even of a snake. I should let him bite me to death

rather than kill him. But it is likely that if God
puts me to that cruel test and permits a snake to
assault me, I may not have the courage to die, but
that the beast in me may assert itself and I may
seek to kill the snake in defending this perishable
body. I admit that my belief has not become so
incarnate in me as to warrant my stating
emphatically that I have shed all fear of snakes so
as to befriend them as I would like to be able to.
It is my implicit belief that snakes, tigers, etc. are
God's answer to the poisonous, wicked, evil
thoughts we harbour.... I believe that all life is one.
Thoughts take definite forms. Tigers and snakes
have kinship with us. They are a warning to us to
avoid harbouring evil, wicked, lustful thoughts. If I
want to rid the earth of venomous beasts and
reptiles, I must rid myself of all venomous
thoughts. I shall not do so if in my impatient
ignorance and in my desire to prolong the existence
of the body I seek to kill the so-called venomous
beasts and reptiles. If in not seeking to defend
myself against such noxious animals, I die, I
should rise again a better and fuller man. With
that faith in me how should I seek to kill a fellow
being in a snake ?

Young India, 14-4-'27

We are living in the midst of death trying to
grope our way to Truth. Perhaps it is as well that
we are beset with danger at every point in our life,
for, in spite of our knowledge of the danger and of
our precarious existence, our indifference to the
source of all life is excelled only by our amazing
arrogance.

Young India, 7-7-'27

All life in the flesh exists by some Himsa. Hence the highest religion has been defined by a negative word Ahimsa. The world is bound in a chain of destruction. In other words Himsa is an inherent necessity for life in the body. That is why a votary of Ahimsa always prays for ultimate deliverance from the bondage of the flesh.

Young India, 4-10-'28

I am painfully aware of the fact that my desire to continue life in the body involves me in constant Himsa. That is why I am becoming growingly indifferent to this physical body of mine. For instance, I know that in the act of respiration I destroy innumerable invisible germs floating in the air. But I do not stop breathing. The consumption of vegetables involves Himsa, but I find that I cannot give them up. Again, there is Himsa in the use of antiseptics, yet I cannot bring myself to discard the use of disinfectants like kerosene, etc. to rid myself of the mosquito pest and the like. I suffer snakes to be killed in the Ashram when it is impossible to catch them and put them out of harm's way. I even tolerate the use of the stick to drive the bullocks in the Ashram. Thus there is no end to Himsa which I directly and indirectly commit. If, as a result of this humble confession of mine, friends choose to give me up as lost, I would be sorry, but nothing will induce me to try to conceal my imperfections in the practice of Ahimsa. All I claim for myself is that I am ceaselessly trying to understand the implications of great ideals like Ahimsa and to practise them in thought, word and deed and that not without a certain measure of success as I think. But I know that I have a long distance yet to cover in this direction.

Young India, 1-11-'28

I believe myself to be saturated with Ahimsa — non-violence. Ahimsa and Truth are as my two lungs. I cannot live without them. But I see every moment, with more and more clearness, the immense power of Ahimsa and the littleness of man. Even the forest dweller cannot be entirely free from violence, in spite of his limitless compassion. With every breath he commits a certain amount of violence. The body itself is a house of slaughter, and, therefore, Moksha and Eternal Bliss consist in perfect deliverance from the body, and therefore, all pleasure, save the joy of Moksha, is evanescent, imperfect. That being the case, we have to drink, in daily life, many a bitter draught of violence.

Young India, 21-10-'26

I verily believe that man's habit of killing man on the slightest pretext has darkened his reason and he gives himself liberties with other life which he would shudder to take if he really believed that God was a God of Love and Mercy. Anyway though for fear of death I may kill tigers, snakes, fleas, mosquitoes and the like, I ever pray for illumination that will shed all fear of death and thus refusing to take life know the better way, for:

Taught by the Power that pities me
I learn to pity them.

Harijan, 9-1-'37

The Cow

The cow is the purest type of sub-human life. She pleads before us on behalf of the whole of the sub-human species for justice to it at the hands of man, the first among all that lives. She seems to speak to us through her eye; : 'You are not appointed over us to kill us and eat our flesh or otherwise ill-treat us, but to be our friend and guardian.'

Young India, 26-6-'24

It is for me a poem of pity. I worship it and I shall defend its worship against the whole world.

Young India, 1-1-'25

34. WHAT IS BRAHMACHARYA

A friend asks : 'What is Brahmacharya ? Is it possible to practise it to perfection? If possible, do you do so ?'

The full and proper meaning of Brahmacharya is search of Brahman. Brahman pervades every being and can therefore be searched by diving into and realizing the inner self. This realization is impossible without complete control of the senses. Brahmacharya thus means control in thought, word and action of all the senses at all times and in all places.

A man or woman completely practising Brahmacharya is absolutely free from passion. Such a one therefore lives nigh unto God, is Godlike.

I have no doubt that it is possible to practise such Brahmacharya in thought, word and action to the fullest extent.

Young India, 5-6-'24

The man, who is wedded to Truth and worships Truth alone, proves unfaithful to her., if he applies his talents to anything else. How then can he minister to the sense? A man, whose activities are wholly consecrated to the realization of Truth, which requires utter selflessness, can have no time for the selfish purpose of begetting children and running a household. Realization of Truth through self-gratification should, after what has been said before, appear a contradiction in terms.

It we look at it from the standpoint of Ahimsa (nonviolence), we find that the fulfilment of Ahimsa is impossible without utter selflessness. Ahimsa means universal love. If a man gives his love to one woman, or a woman to one man, what is there left for all the world besides? It simply means, "We two first, and the devil take all the rest of them." As a faithful wife must be prepared to sacrifice her all for the sake of her husband, and a faithful husband for the sake of his wife, it is clear that such persons cannot rise to the height of universal love, or look upon all mankind as kith and kin. For they have created a boundary wall round their love. The larger their family, the farther are they from universal love. Hence one who would obey the law of Ahimsa cannot marry, not to speak of gratification outside the marital bond.

Then what about people who are already married? Will they never be able to realize Truth? Can they never offer up their all at the altar of humanity ? There is a way out for them. They can behave as if they were not married. Those who have enjoyed this happy condition will be able to bear me out. Many have to my knowledge successfully tried the experiment. If the married couple can think of each other as brother and sister, they are freed for universal service. The very thought that all women in the world are one's sisters, mothers or daughters will at once ennoble a man and snap his chains. The husband and wife do not lose anything here, but only add to their resources and even to their family. Their love becomes free from the impurity of lust and so grows stronger. With the disappearance of this impurity, they can serve each other better, and the occasions for quarrel become fewer. There are more occasions for quarrel, where the love is selfish and bounded.

If the foregoing argument is appreciated, a consideration of the physical benefits of chastity becomes a matter of secondary importance. How foolish it is intentionally to dissipate vital energy in sensual enjoyment! It is a grave misuse to fritter away for physical gratification that which is given to man and woman for the full development of their bodily and mental powers. Such misuse is the root cause of many a disease.

Brahmacharya, like all other observances, must be observed in thought, word and deed. We are told in the Gita, and experience will corroborate the statement, that the foolish man, who appears to control, his body but is nursing evil thoughts in his mind, makes a vain effort. It may be harmful to suppress the body, if the mind is at the same time allowed to go astray. Where the mind wanders, the body must follow sooner or later.

It is necessary here to appreciate a distinction. It is one thing to allow the mind to harbour impure thoughts; it is a different thing altogether if it strays among them in spite of ourselves. Victory will be ours in the end, if we non-co-operate with the mind in its evil wanderings.

We experience every moment of our lives that often while the body is subject to our control, the mind is not. This physical control should never be relaxed, and in addition we must put forth a constant endeavour to bring the mind under control. We can do nothing more, nothing less. If we give way to the mind, the body and the mind will pull different ways, and we shall be false to ourselves. Body and mind may be said to go together, so long as we continue to resist the approach of every evil thought.

The observance of Brahmacharya has been believed to be very difficult, almost impossible. In trying to find a reason for this belief, we see that the term Brahmacharya has been taken in a narrow sense. Mere control of animal passion has been thought to be tantamount to observing Brahmacharya. I feel that this conception is incomplete and wrong. Brahmacharya means control of all the organs of sense. He, who attempts to control only one organ and allows all the others free play, is bound to find his effort futile. To hear suggestive stories with the ears, to see suggestive sights with the eyes, to taste stimulating food with the tongue, to touch exciting things with the hands, and then at the same time expect to control the only remaining organ, is like putting one's hands in a fire, and then expecting to escape being burnt. He, therefore, who is resolved to control the one must be likewise determined to control the rest. I have always felt that much harm has been done by the narrow definition of Brahmacharya. If we practise simultaneous self-control in all directions, the attempt will be scientific and possible of success. Perhaps the palate is the chief sinner. That is why in the Ashram we have assigned to control of the palate a separate place among our observances.

Let us remember the root meaning of Brahma-charya. Charya means course of conduct; Brahma-charya conduct adapted to the search of Brahma, i.e. Truth. From this etymological meaning, arises the special meaning, viz., control of all the senses. We must entirely forget the incomplete definition which restricts itself to the sexual aspect only.

From Yeravda Mandir, Chapter III

35. STEPS TO BRAHMACHARYA

The first step is the realization of its necessity. The next is gradual control of the senses. A Brahmachari must needs control his palate. He must eat to live, and not for enjoyment. He must see only clean things and close his eyes before anything unclean. It is thus a sign of polite breeding to walk with one's eyes towards the ground and not wandering about from object to object. A Brahmachari will likewise hear nothing obscene or unclean, smell no strong, stimulating things. The smell of clean earth is far sweeter than the fragrance of artificial scents and essences. Let the aspirant to Brahmacharya also keep his hands and feet engaged in all the waking hours in healthful activity. Let him also fast occasionally.

The third step is to have clean companions-clean friends and clean books.

The last and not the least is prayer. Let him repeat Ramanama with all his heart regularly everyday, and ask for divine grace.

None of these things are difficult for an average man or woman. They are simplicity itself. But their very simplicity is embarrassing. Where there is a will, the way is simple enough. Men have not the will for it and hence vainly grope. The fact that the world rests on the observance, more or less, of Brahma-charya or restraint, means that it is necessary and practicable.

Young India, 29-4-'26

Many aspirants after Brahmacharya fail, because in the use of their other senses they want to carry on as those who are not Brahmacharis. Their effort is therefore identical with the effort to experience the bracing cold of winter in the scorching summer months. There should be a clear line between the life of a Brahmachari and of one who is not. The resemblance that there is between the two is only apparent. The distinction ought to be clear as daylight. Both use their eyesight, but whereas the Brahmachari uses it to see the glories of God, the other uses it to see the frivolity around him. Both use their ears, but whereas the one hears nothing but praises of God, the other feasts his ears upon ribaldry. Both often keep late hours, but whereas the one devotes them to prayer, the other fritters them away in wild and wasteful mirth. Both feed the inner man, but the one does so only to keep the temple of God in good repair, while the other gorges himself and makes the sacred vessel a stinking gutter. Thus both live as the poles apart, and the distance between them will grow and not diminish with the passage of time.

Brahmacharya means control of the senses in thought, word and deed. Everyday I have been realizing more and more the necessity for restraints of the kind I have detailed above. There is no limit to the possibilities of renunciation, even as there is none to those of Brahmacharya. Such Brahmacharya is impossible of attainment by limited effort. For many, it must remain only as an ideal. An aspirant after Brahmacharya will always be conscious of his shortcomings, will seek out the passions lingering in the innermost recesses of his heart, and will incessantly strive to get rid of them. So long as thought is not under complete control of the will, Brahmacharya in its fulness is absent. Involuntary thought is an affection of the mind; and curbing of thought therefore means curbing of the mind which is even more difficult to curb than the wind. Nevertheless the existence of God within makes even control of the mind possible. Let no one think that it is impossible because it is difficult. It is the highest goal, and it is no wonder that the highest effort should be necessary to attain it.

But it was after coming to India that I realized that such Brahmacharya was impossible to attain merely by human effort. Until then I had been labouring under the delusion that fruit diet alone would enable me to eradicate all passions, and I had flattered myself with the belief that I had nothing more to do.

But I must not anticipate the chapter of my struggles. Meanwhile let me make it clear that those who desire to observe Brahmacharya with a view to realizing God need not despair, provided their faith in God is equal to their confidence in their own effort:

विषया विनिवर्तन्ते निराहारस्य देहिनः ।
रसवर्जं रसोऽप्यस्य परं दृष्ट्वा निवर्तते ॥

(The sense-objects turn away from an abstemious soul, leaving the relish behind. The relish also disappears with the realization of the Highest.)

Therefore His name and His grace are the last resources of the aspirant after Moksha. This truth came to me only after my return to India.

Autobiography (1948), pp.258-60

For me the observance of even bodily Brahmacharya has been full of difficulties. Today I may say that I feel myself fairly safe, but I have yet to achieve complete mastery over thought, which is so essential. Not that the will or effort is lacking, but it is yet a problem to me wherefrom undesirable thoughts spring their insidious invasions. I have no doubt that there is a key to lock out undesirable thoughts, but every one has to find it out for himself. Saints and seers have left their experiences for us, but they have given us no infallible and universal prescription. For perfection or freedom from error comes only from grace, and so seekers after God have left us Mantras, such as Ramanama, hallowed by their own austerities and charged with their purity. Without an unreserved surrender to His grace, complete mastery over thought is impossible. This is the teaching of every great book of religion, and I am realizing the truth of it every moment of my striving after that perfect Brahmacharya.

Autobiography (1948), p.388

I must confess that the observance of the law of continence is impossible without a living faith in God which is living Truth. It is the fashion nowadays to dismiss God from life altogther and insist on the possibility of reaching the highest kind of life without the necessity of a living faith in a living God. I must confess my inability to drive the truth of the law home to those who have no faith in and no need for a Power infinitely higher than themselves. My own experience has led me to the knowledge that fullest life is impossible without an immovable belief in a living law in obedience to which the whole universe moves. A man without that faith is like a drop thrown out of the ocean bound to perish. Every drop in the ocean shares its majesty and has the honour of giving us the ozone of life.

Harijan, 25-4-'36

36. MARRIAGE, A SACRAMENT

Man is, undoubtedly, an artist and creator. Undoubtedly he must have beauty and, therefore, colour. His artistic and creative nature at its best taught him to discriminate, and to know that any conglomeration of colours was no mark of beauty, nor every sense of enjoyment good in itself. His eye for art taught man to seek enjoyment in use-fulness. Thus, he learnt at an early stage of his evolution that he was to eat not for its own sake, as some of us still do, but he should eat to enable him to live. At a later stage, he learnt further that there was neither beauty nor joy in living for its own sake, but that he must live to serve his fellow creatures and through them his Maker. Similarly, when he pondered over the phenomenon of the pleasurableness of sexual union, he discovered that like every other organ of sense this one of generation had its use and abuse. And he saw that its true function, its right use, was to restrict it to generation. Any other use he saw was ugly, and he saw further that it was fraught with very serious consequences, as well to the individual as to the race.

Harijan, 4-4-'36

Human society is a ceaseless growth, an unfoldment in terms of spirituality. If so, it must be based on ever increasing restraint upon the demands of the flesh. Thus, marriage must be considered to be a sacrament imposing discipline upon the partners, restricting them to the physical union only among themselves and for the purpose only of procreation when both the partners desire and are prepared for it.

Young India, 16-9-'26

There can be no two opinions about the necessity of birth-control. But the only method handed down from ages past is self-control or Brahmacharya. It is an infallible sovereign remedy doing good to those who practise it. And medical men will earn the gratitude of mankind, if instead of devising artificial means of birth-control they will find out the means of self-control.

Young India, 12-3-'25

Artificial methods are like putting a premium upon vice. They make man and woman reckless. And respectability that is being given to the methods must hasten the dissolution of the restraints that public opinion puts upon one. Adoption of artificial methods must result in imbecility and nervous prostration. The remedy will be found to be worse than the disease.

Young India, 12-3-'25

It is wrong and immortal to seek to escape the consequences of one's acts. It is good for a person who overeats to have an ache and a fast. It is bad for him to indulge his appetite and then escape the consequence by taking tonics or other medicine. It is still worse for a person to indulge in his animal passions and escape the consequences of his acts.

Nature is relentless and will have full revenge for any such violation of her laws. Moral results can only be produced by moral restraints. All other restraints defeat the very purpose for which they are intended.

Young India, 12-3-'25

The world depends for its existence on the act of generation, and as the world is the playground of God and a reflection of His glory, the act of generation should be controlled for the ordered growth of the world.

Autobiography (1948), p.251

Sex urge is a fine and noble thing. There is nothing to be ashamed of in it. But it is meant only for the act of creation. Any other use of it is a sin against God and humanity.

Harijan, 28-3-'46

It is a sin to bring forth unwanted children, but I think it is a greater sin to avoid the consequences of one's own action. It simply unmans man.

Harijan, 7-9-'35

Man must choose either of the two courses, the upward or the downward; but as he has the brute in him, he will more easily choose the downward course than the upward, especially when the downward course is presented to him in a beautiful garb. Man easily capitulates when sin is presented in the garb of virtue, and that is what Marie Stopes and others are doing.

Harijan, 31-1-'35

37. GOSPEL OF NON-POSSESSION

A seeker after Truth, a follower of the law of love, cannot hold anything against tomorrow. God never provides for the morrow. He never creates more than what is strictly needed from day to day. If, therefore, we repose faith in His Providence, we should rest assured that he will give us every day our daily bread, meaning everything that we require.... Our ignorance or negligence of the Divine law, which gives to man from day to day his daily bread and no more, has given rise to inequalities with all the miseries attendant upon them. The rich have a superfluous store of things which they do not need and which are, therefore, neglected and wasted; while millions starve and are frozen to death for want of them. If each retained possession only of what he needed, no one would be in want and all would live in contentment. As it is, the rich are discontented no less than the poor. The poor man would fain become a millionaire and the millionaire a multimillionaire. The poor are often not satisfied when they get just enough to fill their stomaches; but they are clearly entitled to it and society should make it a point to see that. they get it. The rich must take an initiative in the matter with a view to a universal diffusion of the spirit of contentment. If only they keep their own property within moderate limits the poor will be easily fed; and will learn the lesson of contentment along with the rich. Perfect fulfilment of the ideal of non-possession requires that man should, like the birds, have no roof over his head, no clothing and no stock of food for the morrow. He will, indeed, need his daily bread, but it will be God's business, and not his to provide for it. Only a very few rare soul can attain this ideal, however. We ordinary seekers can only keep it constantly in view, and in the light thereof, critically examine our property and try to reduce it every day. Civilization in the real sense of the term consists not in the multiplication but in the deliberate and voluntary reduction of wants, which promotes real happiness and contentment and increases the capacity for service. One can reduce one's wants by perseverance, and the reduction of wants makes for happiness -- a healthy body and a peaceful mind. From the standpoint of pure truth, the body too is property acquired by the soul. By means of a desire for enjoyment we have created and continue to maintain this encumbrance in the shape of the body. When this desire vanishes, there remains no further need for the body, and man is free from the vicious cycle of births and deaths. The soul is omnipresent; why should she care to be confined within the cagelike body, or do evil and even kill for the sake of that cage? We thus arrive at the ideal of total renunciation and learn to use the body for the purposes of service so long as it exists, so much so that service and not bread becomes with us the staff of life. We eat and drink, sleep and awake for service alone. This brings us real happiness, and the beatific vision in the fulness of time. Let us all examine our possession from this standpoint.

We should remember that non-possession is a principle applicable to thoughts as well as to things. One who fills his brain with useless knowledge violates that inestimable principle. Thoghts which turn us away from God or do not turn us towards Him constitute impediments which one must soon get rid of. In this connection we may consider the definition of knowledge contained in the 13th Chapter of the Gita. We are there told that humility (Amanitvam), etc., constitute knowledge, and all the rest is ignorance. If this is true — and there is no doubt that it is true — much that we hug today as knowledge is ignorance pure and simple and, therefore, only does us harm instead of conferring any benefit. It makes the mind wander and even reduces it to a vacuity, and discontent flourishes in endless ramifications of evil. Needless to say, this is not a plea for inertia. Every moment of our lives should be filled with activity, but that activity should be *Sattvika* tending to truth. One who has consecrated his life to service cannot be idle for a single moment. But one has to learn to distinguish between good activity and evil activity. This discernment goes naturally with a single-minded devotion to service.

From Yeravda Mandir, Chapter VI

Therefore, renounce all and dedicate it to God and then live. The right of living is thus derived from renunciation. It does not say, 'When all do their part of the work I too will do it.' It says, 'Don't bother about others, do your job first, and leave the rest to Him.'

Harijan, 6-3-'37

Jesus, Muhammad, Buddha, Nanak, Kabir, Chaitanya, Shankara, Dayananda, Ramakrishna

were men who exercised an immense influence over
and moulded the character of thousands of men.
The world is the richer for their having lived in it.
And they were all men who deliberately embraced
poverty as their lot.

Speeches and Writings of Mahatma Gandhi, (1933),
p.353

The golden rule... is resolutely to refuse to have
what millions cannot. This ability to refuse will not
descend upon us all of a sudden. The first thing is
to cultivate the mental attitude that will not have
possessions or facilities denied to millions, and the
next immediate thing is to re-arrange our lives as
fast as possible in accordance with that mentality.

Young India, 24-6-'26

If we will take care of today, God will take care
of the morrow.

Young India, 13-10-'21

38. WORK AS WORSHIP

'Brahma created His people with the duty of
sacrifice laid upon them, and said: "By this do you
flourish. Let it be the fulfiller of all your desires,"
'He who eats without performing this sacrifice, eats
stolen bread' -- thus says the Gita. 'Earn thy bread
by the sweat of thy brow,' says the Bible. Sacrifices
may be of many kinds. One of them may well be
bread labour. If all laboured for their bread and no
more, then there would be enough food and enough
leisure for all. Then there would be no cry of over-
population, no disease, and no such misery as we
see around. Such labour will be the highest form of
sacrifice. Men will no doubt do many other things,

either through their bodies or through their minds, but all this will be labour of love, for the common good. There will then be no rich and no poor, none high and none low, no touchable and no untouchable.

Harijan, 29-6-'35

This may be an unattainable ideal. But we need not, therefore, cease to strive for it. Even if, without fulfilling the whole law of sacrifice, that is, the law of our being, we performed physical labour enough for our daily bread, we should go a long way towards the ideal.

Harijan, 29-6-'35

If we did so, our wants would be minimized, our food would be simple. We should then eat to live, not live to eat. Let anyone who doubts the accuracy of this proposition try to sweat for his bread, he will derive the greatest relish from the productions of his labour, improve his health, and discover that many things he took were superfluities.

Harijan, 29-6-'35

May not men earn their bread by intellectual labour? No. The needs of the body must be supplied by the body. 'Render unto Caesar that which is Caesar's' perhaps applies here as well. Mere mental, that is, intellectual labour is for the soul and is its own satisfaction. It should never demand payment. In the ideal State, doctors, lawyers and the like will work solely for the benefit of society, not for self.

Obedience to the law of bread labour will bring about a silent revolution in the structure of society. Men's triumph will consist in substituting the struggle for existence by the struggle for mutual service. The law of the brute will be replaced by the law of man.

Harijan, 29-6-'35

Return to the villages means a definite voluntary recognition of the duty of bread labour and all it connotes.

Harijan, 29-6-'35

God of Himself seeks for His seat the heart of him who serves his fellowmen. Such was Abu Ben Adhem. He served his fellowmen and therefore his name topped the list of those who served God.

Young India, 24-9-'25

But who are the suffering and the woe-begone? The suppressed and the poverty-stricken. He who would be a *bhakta,* therefore, must serve these by body, soul and mind. He who does not even condescend to exert his body to the extent of spinning for the sake of the poor and trots out lame excuses does not know the meaning of service. He who spins before the poor inviting them to do likewise serves God as no one else does. "He who gives Me even a trifle as a fruit or a flower or even a leaf in the spirit of *bhakti* is my servant", says the Lord in the Bhagavadgita. And He hath His footstool where live "the humble, the lowliest and lost". Spinning, therefore, for such is the greatest prayer, the greatest worship, the greatest sacrifice.

Young India, 24-9-'25

Q: Would it not be better for a man to give the time he spends on the worship of God to the service of the poor? And should not true service make devotional worship unnecessary for such a man ?

A: I sense mental laziness as also agnosticism in this question. The biggest of Karmayogis never give up devotional songs or worship. Idealistically it may be said that true service of others is itself worship and that such devotees do not need to spend any time in songs, etc. As a matter of fact, *Bhajans,* etc. are a help to true service and keep the remembrance of God fresh in the heart of the devotee.

Harijan, 13-10-'46

No work that is done in His name and dedicated to Him is small. All work when so done assumes equal merit. A scavenger who works in His service shares equal distinction with a king who uses his gifts in His name and as a mere trustee.

Young India, 25-11-'26

I cannot imagine anything nobler or more national than that for, say, one hour in the day, we should all do the labour that the poor must do, and thus identify ourselves with them and through them with all mankind. I cannot imagine better worship of God than that in His name I should labour for the poor even as they do.

Young India, 20-10-'21

There can never be too much emphasis placed on work. I am simply repeating the gospel taught by the Gita where the lord says, 'If I did not remain ever at work sleeplessly, I should set a wrong example to mankind.'

Harijan, 2-11-'35

We should be ashamed of resting or having a square meal so long as there is one able-bodied man or woman without work or food

Young India, 6-10-'21

Service is not possible unless it is rooted in love or Ahimsa. True love is boundless like the ocean and rising and swelling within one spreads itself out and crossing all boundaries and frontiers envelops the whole world. This service is again impossible without bread labour, otherwise described in the Gita as Yajna. It is only when a man or woman has done bodily labour for the sake of service that he or she has the right to live.

Young India, 20-9-'28

39. SARVODAYA

This body... has been given to us only in order that we may serve all Creation with it. And, therefore, says the Gita, he who eats without offering Yajna eats stolen food. Every single act of one who would lead a life of purity should be in the nature of Yajna*. Yajna having come to us with our birth, we are debtors all our lives, and thus for ever bound to serve the universe. And even as bondslave receives food, clothing and so on from the master whom he serves, so should we gratefully accept such gifts as may be assigned to us by the Lord of the universe. What we receive must be called a gift; for as debtors we are entitled to no consideration for the discharge of our obligations.

---

* 'What Yajna means has been explained by Gandhiji in an earlier paragraph. He says: "Yajna means an act directed to the welfare of others, done without desiring any return for it, whether of a temporal or spiritual nature. 'Act' here must be taken in its widest sense, and includes thought and word, as well as deed. 'Others' embraces not only humanity, but all life. Therefore, and from the standpoint of Ahimsa it is not a Yajna to sacrifice lower animals even with a view to the service of humanity."

Therefore we may not blame the Master, if we fail to get it. Our body is His to be cherished or cast away according to His will. This is not a matter for complaint or even pity; on the contrary, it is a natural and even a pleasant and desirable state, if only we realize our proper place in God's scheme. We do indeed need strong faith, if we would experience this supreme bliss. "Do not worry in the least about yourself, leave all worry to God," ...this appears to be the commandment in all religions.

This need not frighten any one. He who devotes himself to service with a clear conscience will day by day grasp the necessity for it in greater measure, and will continually grow richer in faith. The path of service can hardly be trodden by one, who is not prepared to renounce self-interest, and to recognize the conditions of his birth. Consciously or unconsciously every one of us does render some service or other. If we cultivate this habit of doing this service deliberately, our desire for service will steadily grow stronger, and will make not only for our own happiness but that of the world at large.

From Yeravda Mandir, Chapter XIV

A votary of Ahimsa cannot subscribe to the utilitarian formula (of the greatest good of the greatest number). He will strive for the greatest good of all and die in the attempt to realize the ideal. He will, therefore, be willing to die, so that the others may live. He will serve himself with the rest, by himself dying. The greatest good of all inevitably includes the good of the greatest number, and therefore, he and the utilitarian will converge in many points in their career but there does come a time when they must part company, and even work in opposite directions. The utilitarian to be logical will never sacrifice himself.

Young India, 9-12-'26

I do not believe... that an individual may gain spiritually and those who surround him suffer. I believe in Advaita. I believe in the essential unity of man and, for that matter, of all that lives. Therefore, I believe that if one man gains spiritually, the whole world gains with him and, if one man falls, the whole world falls to that extent.

Young India, 4-12-'24

There is not a single virtue which aims at, or is content with, the welfare of the individual alone. Conversely, there is not a single offence which does not, directly or indirectly, affect many others besides the actual offender. Hence, whether an individual is good or bad is not merely his own concern, but really the concern of the whole community, nay, of the whole world.

Ethical Religion (1927), p.55

A life of service must be one of humility. He, who would sacrifice his life for others, has hardly time to reserve for himself a place in the sun. Inertia must not be mistaken for humility, as it has been in Hinduism. True humility means most strenuous and constant endeavour entirely directed to the service of humanity. God is continuously in action without resting for a single moment. If we would serve Him or become one with Him, our activity must be as unwearied as His.

From Yeravda Mandir, Chapter XII

There may be momentary rest in store for the drop which is separated from the ocean, but not for the drop in the ocean, which knows no rest. The same is the case with ourselves. As soon as we become one with the ocean in the shape of God, there is no more rest for us, nor indeed do we need rest any longer. Our very sleep is action. For we sleep with the thought of God in our hearts. This restlessness constitutes true rest. This never-ceasing agitation holds the key to peace ineffable. This supreme state of total surrender is difficult to describe, but not beyond the bounds of human experience. It has been attained by many dedicated souls, and may be attained by ourselves as well.

From Yeravda Mandir, Ch. XII

40. ETHICS OF THE ATOM BOMB

It has been suggested by American friends that the atom bomb will bring in Ahimsa as nothing else can. It will, if it is meant that its destructive power will so disgust the world that it will turn it away from violence for the time being. This is very like a man glutting himself with dainties to the point of nausea and turning away from them only to return with redoubled zeal after the effect of nausea is well over. Precisely in the same manner will the world return to violence with renewed zeal after the effect of disgust is worn out.

Often does good come out of evil. But that is God's, not man's plan. Man knows that only evil can come out of evil, as good out of good.

That atomic energy, though harnessed by American scientists and army men for destructive purposes, may be utilized by other scientists for humanitarian purposes is undoubtedly within the realm of possibility. But that is not what was meant by my American friends. They were not so simple as to put a question which connoted an obvious truth. An incendiary uses fire for his destructive and nefarious purpose, a housewife makes daily use of it in preparing nourishing food for mankind.

So far as I can see, the atomic bomb has deadened the finest feeling that has sustained mankind for ages. There used to be the so-called laws of war which made it tolerable. Now we know the naked truth. War knows no law except that of might. The atom bomb brought an empty victory to the Allied arms but it resulted for the time being in destroying the soul of Japan. What has happened to the soul of the destroying nation is yet too early to see. Forces of Nature act in a mysterious manner. We can but solve the mystery by deducing the unknown result from the known results of similar events. A slaveholder cannot hold a slave without putting himself or his deputy in the cage holding the slave. Let no one run away with the idea that I wish to put in a defence of Japanese misdeeds in pursuance of Japan's unworthy ambiton. The difference was only one of degree. I assume that Japan's greed was more unworthy. But the greater unworthiness conferred no right on the less unworthy of destroying without mercy men, women and children of Japan in a particular area.

The moral to be legitimately drawn from the supreme tragedy of the bomb is that it will not be destroyed by counter-bombs even as violence cannot be by counter-violence. Mankind has to get out of violence only through non-violence. Hatred can be overcome only by love. Counter-hatred only increases the surface as well as the depth of hatred. I am aware that I am repeating what I have many times stated before and practised to the best of my ability and capacity. What I first stated was itself nothing new. It was as old as the hills. Only I recited no copy-book maxim but definitely announced what I believed in every fibre of my being. Sixty years of practice in various walks of life has only enriched the belief which experience of friends has fortified. It is, however, the central truth by which one can stand alone without flinching. I believe in what Max Muller said years ago, namely, that truth needed to be repeated as long as there were men who disbelieved it.

Harijan, 7-7-'46

41. PEACE ON EARTH

It is my firm opinion that Europe today represents not the spirit of God or Christianity but the spirit of Satan. And Satan's successes are the greatest when he appears with the name of God on his lips. Europe is today only nominally Christian. It is really worshipping Mammon. 'It is easier for a camel to pass through the eye of a needle than for a rich man to enter the Kingdom.' Thus really spoke Jesus Christ. His so-called followers measure their moral progress by their material possessions.

Young India, 8-9-'20

By all means drink deep of the fountains that are given to you in the Sermon on the Mount, but then you will have to take sackcloth and ashes. The teaching of the Sermon was meant for each and every one of us. You cannot serve both God and Mammon. God the Compassionate and the

Merciful, Tolerance incarnate, allows Mammon to have his nine days' wonder. But I say to you... fly from that self-destroying but destructive show of Mammon.

Young India, 8-12-'27

A time is coming when those, who are in the mad rush today of multiplying their wants, vainly thinking that they add to the real substance, real knowledge of the world, will retrace their steps and say: 'What have we done?' Civilizations have come and gone, and in spite of all our vaunted progress I am tempted to ask again and again 'To what purpose?' Wallace, a contemporary of Darwin, has said the same thing. Fifty years of brilliant inventions and discoveries, he has said, have not added one inch to the moral height of mankind. So said a dreamer and visionary if you will — Tolstoy. So said Jesus, and Buddha, and Muhammad, whose religion is being denied and falsified in my own country today.

Young India, 8-12-'27

Not to believe in the possibility of permanent peace is to disbelieve in the Godliness of human nature. Methods hitherto adopted have failed because rock-bottom sincerity on the part of those who have striven has been lacking. Not that they have realized this lack. Peace is unattained by part performance of conditions, even as a chemical combination is impossible without complete fulfil- ment of the conditions of attainment thereof. If the recognized leaders of mankind who have control over the engines of destruction were wholly to renounce their use, with full knowledge of its implications, permanent peace can be obtained. This is clearly impossible without the great powers

of the earth renouncing their imperialistic design.
This again seems impossible without great nations
ceasing to believe in soul-destroying competition
and to desire to multiply wants and, therefore,
increase their material possessions. It is my
conviction that the root of the evil is want of a
living faith in a living God. It is a first-class
human tragedy that peoples of the earth who claim
to believe in the message of Jesus whom they
describe as the Prince of Peace show little of that
belief in actual practice. It is painful to see sincere
Christian divines limiting the scope of Jesus'
message, to select individuals. I have been taught
from my childhood and tested the truth by
experience that the primary virtues of mankind are
possible of cultivation by the meanest of the human
species. It is this undoubted universal possibility
that distinguishes the humans from the rest of
God's creation. If even one nation were
unconditionally to perform the supreme act of
renunciation, many of us would see in our lifetime
visible peace established on earth.

Harijan, 18-6-'38

If the best minds of the world have not imbibed
the spirit of non-violence, they would have to meet
gangsterism in the orthodox way. But that would
only show that we have not gone far beyond the
law of the jungle, that we have not yet learnt to
appreciate the heritage that God has given us,
that, in spite of the teaching of Christianity which
is 1,900 years old and of Hinduism and Buddhism
which are older, and even of Islam, we have not
made much headway as human beings. But whilst
I would understand the use of force by those who
have not the spirit of nonviolence in them I would

have those who know non-violence to throw their whole weight in demonstrating that even gangsterism has to be met with non-violence.

Harijan, 10-12-'38

Brute force has been the ruling factor in the world for thousands of years, and mankind has been reaping its bitter harvest all along, as he who runs may read. There is little hope of anything good coming out of it in the future. If light came out of darkness, then alone can love emerge from hatred.

Satyagraha in South Africa, p.289

42. OBITER DICTA

Death

Why should we be upset when children or young men or old men die? Not a moment passes when some one is not born or is not dead in this world. We should feel the stupidity of rejoicing in a birth and lamenting a death. Those who believe in the soul – and what Hindu, Mussalman or Parsee is there who does not know that the soul never dies. The souls of the living as well as of the dead are all one. The eternal processes of creation and destruction are going on ceaselessly. There is nothing in it for which we might give ourselves up to joy or sorrow. Even if we extend the idea of relationship only to our countrymen and take all the births in the country as taking place in our family, how many births shall we celebrate ? If we weep for all the deaths in our country, the tears in our eyes would never dry. This train of thought should help us to get rid of all fear of death.

Young India, 13-10-'21

Birth and death are not two different states, but they are different aspects of the same state. There is as little reason to deplore the one as there is to be pleased over the other.

Young India, 20-11-'24

Immortality

I believe in the immortality of the soul. I would like to give you the analogy of the ocean. The ocean is composed of drops of water, each drop is an entity and yet it is part of the whole, 'the one and the many'. In this ocean of life we are all little drops. My doctrine means that I must identify myself with life, with everything that lives, that I must share the majesty of life in the presence of God. The sum total of this life is God.

India's Case for Swaraj (1932), p.245

Insurance

I had thought that life insurance implied fear and want of faith in God... In getting my life insured I had robbed my wife and children of their self-reliance. Why should they be not expected to take care of themselves? What happened to the families of the numberless poor in the world? Why should I not count myself as one of them? What reason had I to assume that death would claim me earlier than the others? After all the real protector was neither I nor my brother but God Almighty.

Autobiography (1948), pp. 320-21

Means and Ends

They say, 'means are after all means.' I would say, 'means are after all everything.' As the means so the end. There is no wall of separation between the means and the end. Indeed the Creator has given us control (and that too very limited) over means, none over the end. Realization of the goal is in exact proportion to that of the means. This is a proposition that admits of no exception.

Young India, 17-7-'24

Politics

To see the universal and all-pervading spirit of Truth face to face one must be able to love the meanest of creation as oneself. And a man who aspires after that cannot afford to keep out of any field of life. That is why my devotion to Truth has drawn me into the field of politics; and I can say without the slightest hesitation, and yet in all humility, that those who say that religion has nothing to do with politics do not know what religion means.

Autobiography (1948), p.615

For me, politics bereft of religion are absolute dirt, ever to be shunned. Politics concern nations and that which concerns the welfare of nations must be one of the concerns of a man who is religiously inclined, in other words a seeker after God and Truth. For me God and Truth are convertible terms, and if anyone told me that God was a God of untruth or a God of torture I would decline to worship Him. Therefore, in politics also we have to establish the Kingdom of Heaven.

Young India, 18-6-'25

I could not be leading a religious life unless I identified myself with the whole of mankind, and that I could not do unless I took part in politics. The whole gamut of man's activities today constitutes an indivisible whole. You cannot divide social, economic, political and purely religious work into watertight compartments. I do not know any religion apart from human activity. It provides a moral basis to all other activities which they would otherwise lack, reducing life to a maze of 'sound and fury signifying nothing'.

Harijan, 24-12-'38

Predestination

Q : Are the time, place and manner of death predestined by the Almighty for each individual? If so, why worry even if we are ill?

A: I do not know whether time, place and the manner of death are predestined. All I do know is that 'not a blade of grass moves but by His will'. This too I know hazily. What is hazy today will be clear tomorrow or the day after by prayerful waiting. Let this however be quite clear. The Almighty is not a person like us. He or It is the greatest living Force or Law in the world. Accordingly He does not act by caprice, nor does that Law admit of any amendment or improvement. His will is fixed and changeless, everything else changes every second. Surely, it does not follow from the doctrine of predestination that we may not 'worry' in the care of ourselves even if we are ill. Indifference to illness is a crime greater than that of falling ill. There is no end to the effort to do better today than yesterday. We have to 'worry' and find out why we are or have become ill. Health, not 'illth', is the law of nature. Let us investigate the law of nature and obey it, if we will not be ill or, if having fallen ill, will be restored.

Harijan, 28-7-'46

Progress

Evolution is always experimental. All progress is gained through mistakes and their rectification. No good comes fully fashioned, out of God's hand, but has to be carved out through repeated experiments and repeated failures by ourselves. This is the law of individual growth. The same law controls social and political evolution also. The right to err, which means the freedom to try experiments, is the universal condition of all progress.

Speeches and Writings of Mahatma Gandhi (1933), p. 245

The nations have progressed both by evolution and revolution. The one is as necessary as the other. Death, which is an eternal verity, is revolution as birth and after is slow and steady evolution. Death is as necessary for man's growth as life itself. God is the greatest revolutionary the world has ever known or will know. He sends storms where a moment ago there was calm. He levels down mountains which He builds with exquisite care and infinite patience. I do watch the sky and it fills me with awe and wonder. In the serene blue sky, both of India and England, I have seen clouds gathering and bursting with a fury which has struck me dumb. History is more a record of wonderful revolutions than the so-called ordered progress.

Young India, 2-2-'22

Rebirth

I am a believer in previous births and rebirths. All our relationships are the result of the Sanskaras we carry from previous births. God's laws are inscrutable and are the subject of endless search. No one will fathom them.

Harijan, 18-8-'40

Religious Education

I do not believe that the State can concern itself or cope with religious instruction. I believe that religious education must be the sole concern of religious associations. Do not mix up religion and ethics. I believe that fundamental ethics is common to all religions. Teaching of fundamental ethics is undoubtedly a function of the State. By religion I have not in mind fundamental ethics but what goes by the name of denominationalism. We have suffered enough from State-aided religion and a State-church. A society or group, which depends partly or wholly on State aid for the existence of its religion, does not deserve or, better still, does not have any religion worth the name. I do not need to give any illustrations in support of this obvious truth as it is to me.

Harijan, 31-8-'47

Religious Ideal

...The very virtue of a religious ideal lies in the fact that it cannot be completely realized in the flesh. For a religious ideal must be proved by faith, and how can faith have play if perfection could be attained by the spirit while it was still surrounded by its 'earthly vesture of decay'? Where would there be scope for its infinite expansion which is its essential characteristic? Where would be room for that constant striving, that ceaseless quest after the ideal that is the basis of all spiritual progress, if mortals could reach the perfect state while still in the body ? If such easy perfection in the body was possible, all we would have to do would be simply to follow a cut and dry model. Similarly if a perfect code of conduct were possible for all there would be no room for a diversity of faiths and religions because there would be only one standard religion which everybody would have to follow.

Young India, 22-11-'28

The virtue of an ideal consists in its boundlessness. But although religious ideals must thus, from their nature, remain unattainable by imperfect human beings, although by virtue of their boundlessness they may seem ever to recede further away from us, the nearer we go to them, still they are closer to us than our very hands and feet because we are more certain of their reality and truth than even of our own physical being. This faith in one's ideals alone constitutes true life, in fact, it is man's all in all.

Young India, 22-11-'28

Rights

The true source of rights is duty. If we all discharge our duties, rights will not be far to seek. If leaving duties unperformed we run after rights, they will escape us like a will-o'-the-wisp. The more we pursue them, the farther will they fly. The same teaching has been embodied by Krishna in the immortal words: 'Action alone is thine. leave thou the fruit severely alone.' Action is duty; fruit is the right.

Young India, 8-1-'25

Secrecy

I have come to regard secrecy as a sin.... If we realized the presence of God as witness to all we say and do, we would not have anything to conceal from any body on earth. For we would not think unclean thoughts before our Maker, much less speak them. It is uncleanness that seeks secrecy and darkness. The tendency of human nature is to hide dirt; we do not want to see or touch dirty things; we want to put them out of sight. And so must it be with our speech. I would suggest that we should avoid even thinking thoughts we would hide from the world.

Young India, 22-12-'20

Sin

I do not seek redemption from the consequences of my sin; I seek to be redeemed from sin itself or rather from the very thought of sin. Until I have attained that end I shall be content to be restless.

Mahatma Gandhi's Ideas (1930), p.70

A sinner is equal to the saint in the eye of God. Both will have equal justice, and both an equal opportunity either to go forward or to go backward. Both are His children, His creation. A saint who considers himself superior to a sinner forfeits his sainthood and becomes worse than the sinner, who, unlike the proud saint, knows not what he is doing.

Harijan, 14-10-'33

I have made the frankest admission of my many sins. But I do not carry their burden on my shoulders. If I am journeying Godward, as I feel I am, it is safe with me. For I feel the warmth of the sunshine of His presence. My austerities, fastings and prayers are, I know, of no value, if I rely upon them for reforming me. But they have an inestimable value, if they represent, as I hope they do, the yearnings of a soul striving to lay his weary head in the lap of his Maker.

Harijan, 18-4-'36

Spiritualism

I never receive communications from the spirits of the dead. I have no evidence warranting a disbelief in the possibility of such communications. But I do strongly disapprove of the practice of holding or attempting to hold such communications. They are often deceptive and are products of the imagination. The practice is harmful both to the medium and the spirits, assuming the possibility of such communica-tions. It attracts and ties to the earth the spirit so invoked whereas its effort should be to detach itself from the earth, and rise higher. A spirit is not necessarily purer because it is disembodied. It takes with it most of the frailties to which it was liable when on earth. Information or advice, therefore, given by it need not be true or sound. That the spirit likes communications with those on earth is no matter for pleasure. On the contrary it should be weaned from such unlawful attachment. So much for the harm done to the spirits.

Young India, 12-9-'29

As for the medium, it is a matter of positive knowledge with me that all those within my experience have been deranged or weak-brained and disabled for practical work whilst they were holding, or thought they were holding, such

communications. I can recall no friend of mine who
having held such communications had benefited in
any way.

Young India, 12-9-'29

Superstition

Superstitions and undesirable things go as soon
as we begin to live the correct life. I concern myself
not with belief but with asking to do the right
thing. As soon as they do it, their belief rights
itself.

Young India, 11-8-'27

NON-ENGLISH WORDS WITH
THEIR MEANINGS

Abhyasa – repetition; practice; study

Abu Ben Adhem – a saintly Muslim character, the creation of Leigh Hunt's poetic imagination, who is represented as one who, though he was content to be known merely as a lover of his fellowmen, found his name in the recording angel's book leading the list of those who loved the Lord

Adi Parva – first book of the Hindu epic, Mahabharata Advaita-Hindu philosophy of Non-dualism

Advaitist-a believer in non-dualism

Agiari-Zoroastrian fire-temple

Ahimsa-non-violence

Ahriman – Spirit of Evil, in Zoroastrian religion

Ahurmazd – Zoroastrian name of God

Akash – ether; sky

Allah – Muslim name of God

Amanitvam – humility

Ananda – joy

Anekantavada – belief in many doctrines; scepticism

Anekantavadi-a believer in many doctrines; a sceptic

Arya Samaj – a Hindu reformist organization founded by Swami Dayananda Saraswati in the last century

Ashram – abode of a spiritual teacher; hermitage; one of the four stages of life according to Hinduism

Avatara – incarnation of God

Ayodhya – capital of the kingdom of Rama, the epic hero

Bansi-flute

Bhagavadgita – The Song Celestial, a highly philosophical poem of 700 verses which occurs in the

Mahabharata and in which Krishna, incarnate God, discourses on eternal verities

Bhajan – hymn; singing of hymns

Bhakta-a devotee

Bhakti-devotion

Brahma – Hindu name of God, the Creator

Brahmachari-a celibate; one who lives a life of self-restraint

Brahmacharya-celibacy; continence; life of self-restraint

Brahman-God

Brahmana – member of the first (priestly) caste among Hindus

Brahmaputra – a river of north-eastern India

Chaitanya – Bengali religious reformer of the 15th century A. D. who preached *Bhakti* or devotion to God

Chapati-thin, flat cake made of floor

Charya-conduct; practice

Chit-knowledge

Dada Hormazda – Zoroastrian name of God

Daridranarayana-God in the form of the poor

Dasharatha-King of Ayodhya and father of Rama, the epic hero

Dayananda – Swami Dayananda Saraswati, founder of the *Arya Samaj*

Devadhideva – God of Gods

Deva, Devata-god

Dharma – religion; law of one's being; duty

Dvaita-Hindu philosophy of Dualism

Dvaitism-doctrine of Dualism

Ganga-well-known sacred river of northern India

Gayatri-sacred Vedic Mantra (or formula) which is recited by orthodox Hindus in their daily worship

Gita-same as Bhagavadgita

Guru – teacher; religious preceptor

Hanuman – monkey-chief of the epic Ramayana, whom Hindus venerate as a divinity

Harishchandra – an ancient Hindu king who sacrificed his all for the sake of truth

Himsa – violence

Imam Hasan and Imam Husain – saintly sons of Hazrat Ali, son-in-law of Prophet Muhammad

Ishwara – Hindu name for God

Islam – religion founded by Prophet Muhammad

Jainism – an ancient religion of India propagated by 24 Tirthankars or Saviours, the first of whom was Rishabha and the last Mahavira, who was a contemporary of Buddha in the 6th century B. C. One of the cardinal doctrines of Jainism is Ahimsa or Non-violence

Janaka – an ancient Hindu king who was a great philosopher

Janmashtami – birthday of Shri Krishna, Hindu incarnation of God, to whom the Bhagavadgita or *The Song Celestial* is ascribed

Japa – silent repetition

Jehova – Hebrew name of God

Judaism – the religion of the Jews

Kabir – poet-saint of northern India who lived in the 15th century A. D. and who preached the essential unity of the Godhead and harmony of all religions

Kalma – a Muslim formula of prayer

Karmayogi – a follower of the path of selfless action

Khuda – Muslim name for God

Koran – Book of Revelation of Islam

Krishna – central figure of the epic, Mahabharata, who is venerated by Hindus as God incarnate

Lila-play

Mahabharata – Hindu epic of about 1,00,000 verses, the central theme of which is the great war between the Pandavas and their cousins the Kauravas, who were rival claimants to the throne of Hastinapur (ancient Delhi)

Mandir – Hindu temple

Mantra – a sacred text or formula

Manu – ancient Hindu law-giver

Maya – illusion; divine power

Moksha – liberation; freedom from birth and death

Namaz-daily prayer of Muslims

Nanak – founder of Sikhism (1469-1538 or 1539 A. D.)

Narasinha Mehta-poet-saint of Gujarat who lived in the 15th century

Nirvana – final emancipation from sway of passions; Buddhist goal of life

Niyamas – rules of conduct

Omkar – the sacred and mystic syllable *Om*

Paramatma – the Supreme Self or God

Pariahs-'untouchables' among Hindus

Prahlad – son of a mythological demon-king and devotee of God Vishnu, who faced dreadful ordeals in defence of his faith, remaining steadfast to the end

Puranas – Hindu mythological books

Rahaman – Muslim name of God

Rahim – Muslim name of God

Rama, Ramachandra – hero of the epic, Ramayana, who is regarded as an incarnation of God by Hindus

Ramakrishna – Bengali saint (1836-86 A.D.) who taught the oneness of the Godhead and the basic harmony of all religions. The Ramakrishna Mission is named after him

Ramanama – name of Rama (i.e. God)

Ramayana – Hindu epic which relates the story of the abduction of Sita, wife of Rama, prince of Ayodhya, by Ravana, demon-king of Lanka, and her rescue by Rama after the destruction of the demon

Ramanuja – Hindu philosopher-saint of the 11th century A. D. who was an exponent of Vishishtadvaita or qualified Monism

Sanatani – a follower of orthodox Hinduism

Sannyasa – renunciation of worldly ties

Sanskaras – innate tendencies inherited from past lives

Sarvodqya – welfare of all

Sat – truth; that which exists

Sat-Chit-Ananda – Truth-Knowledge-Bliss

Sattvika – endowed with goodness; virtuous

Satya – truth

Satyagraha – recourse to truth-force or soul-force

Satyavan – husband of Savitri, heroine of well-known mythological episode. She wins back his life from Yama, the god of death

Savitri – heroine of the Satyavan-Savitri episode

Shankara – Hindu philosopher of the 8th century A. D. who was an exponent of Advaita or Absolute Non-Dualism; a name of the Deity

Shankaracharya – same as Shankara; also a member of the order of monks founded by Shankara

Shastra – Hindu scripture

Shastri – one versed in scriptures

Shuddhi – lit. "purification"; conversion to Hindu faith

Shudra-member of the fourth of menial caste among Hindus

Sthitaprajna – one who is firmly established in transcendental knowledge

Surdas – blind Hindi poet-saint of northern India who lived in the 16th century A. D.

Syadvada – philosophy of "probability" in matters of perception by the senses; a form of scepticism. Which is professed by a section of Jain thinkers

Syadvadi – a believer in Syadvada

Tabligh – propaganda and conversion to Islam

Tapas – penance; religious austerity

Trappist – an order of Christian monks who observe the vow of silence

Tulsidas – Hindi poet of northern India who lived in the 16th century A.D. and whose work *Ramacharitamanasa,* recounting the story of the epic hero, Rama, has become universally popular with Hindus

Upanishads – ancient philosophical treatises which are believed by Hindus to contain revealed truth

Vairagya – aversion to worldly life

Vaishnava – a devotee of God Vishnu, the "Preserver" among the Hindu Trinity

Varnashrama – four-fold division of Hindu society

Vedas – most ancient scriptures of Hindus which are believed to embody revealed truth

Vedic – belonging to Vedas

Vishnu – the "Preserver" among Hindu Trinity

Vyasa – compiler of the Vedas and author of the Mahabharata

Yajna – sacrifice

Yamuna – a river of northern India, hallowed by its associations with Krishna, the Hindu incarnation

Zend Avesta – Zoroastrian scripture

Zoroaster – founder of Zoroastrian religion which is professed by the Parsees of India. He is also known as Zarathustra or Zerdusht

SOURCES

An Autobiography or the Story of My Experiments with Truth by M. K. Gandhi. Navajivan Publishing House, Ahmedabad-14, Edi. 1948.

The Bombay Chronicle, daily newspaper published at Bombay

Ethical Religion by Mahatma Gandhi. S. Ganesan, Madras, 1927

From Yeravda Mandir by M. K. Gandhi. Navajivan Publishing House, Ahmedabad-14, Edi. 1945,

Harijan, weekly journal, formerly edited by Mahatma Gandhi and others. Now defunct. Published at the Navajivan Publishing House, Ahmedabad-14

Hind Swaraj or *Indian Home Rule* by M. K. Gandhi, Navajivan Publishing House, Ahmedabad-14. Edi. 1946.

Mahatma Gandhi, Ganesh & Co., Madras, 1918

Mahatma Gandhi's Ideas by C. F. Andrews, Allen and Unwin, London, 1930

The Modern Review, monthly journal published at Calcutta

The Nation's Voice, Navajivan Publishing House, Ahmedabad-14. Edi. 1947.

Satyagraha in South Africa by M. K. Gandhi. Navajivan Publishing House, Ahmedabad-14.

Speeches and Writings of Mahatma Gandhi, G. A. Natesan, Madras (4th Edi.), 1933

Young India, weekly journal, was edited by Mahatma Gandhi (1919-1932) and published at Ahmedabad

INDEX

ABHYASA, 19

Abu Ben Adhem, 47, 135

Action, desireless, 98, 100, 151

Adam, 97

Adiparva, 96

Advaita, Advaitism, 9

Agiari, 87

Ahimsa, 2, 9, 12, 17, 32, 34-38, 55, 63, 74, 93, 102-103, 115-116, 120, 136-138, 140

Ahriman, 53

Ahuramazda, 42, 53

Akash, 111

Allah, 10, 50, 62, 109, 111

Amanitvam, 132

Ananda, 18

Andrews, C. F., 51

Anekantavada, 9

Anekantavadi, 9

Anglo-Indians, 70

Animals, animal sacrifice, 76

Antiseptics, 117

Art, artist, 104-107

Arya Samaj, 72

Atheism, atheist, 7, 10-12, 39

Atom bomb, 10-141

Authority, 92-93

Avataras, 74

Ayodhya, 109

BANSI, 8

Beauty, 104-107

Beef-eating, 69

Bhagavadgita, see Gita

Bhajans, 136

Bhakta, Bhakti, 20, 47, 48, 95, 99, 135,

Bible, 60, 67-74, 77-78, 81-82, 133

Birth, 145-146

Birth-control, 128-129

Blavatsky, Madame, 43

Bliss, Eternal, 18, 118

Body-labour, 47, 103

Bose, Sir J. C., 5

Bradlaugh, Charles, 12, 39

Brahma, 123, 133

Brahmachari, Brahmacharya, 14, 74, 119, 123-129

Brahman, 10, 95, 119

Brahmana, 66

Brahmaputra, 65

Bread-labour, 25, 48, 133-135

Brotherhood, 3, 62, 79
Buddha, 44-45, 76-77
Buddhism, 73, 76, 79, 144

CAESAR, 134
Calamity, 22
Chaitanya, 91, 132
Chastity, 121
China, 67
Chit, 18
Christ, see Jesus Christ
Christianity, 53, 61-62,
    67-69, 72, 76, 78-80,
    142, 144
Church, 61, 81, 85, 86, 87
Civilization, 58, 131, 143
Communion with God, 24
Conscience, 8, 14, 27, 65
Continence, 126
Control, of the palate, 123
Control, of the senses,
    119, 120-126
Conversion, 61
Cow, 73, 118-119
Cowardice, 53
Cross, 84

DADA HORMUZDA, 10
Daridranarayan, 24-26
Darwin, 143
Dasharatha, 84, 109
Dayananda, 132
Death, 6, 20, 22, 110, 111,
    118, 145-146, 148-149

Denominationalism, 150
Desirelessness, 104
Deva-Devata, 81
Devadhideva, 81
Devotee, Devotion, 19, 48,
    49, 88, 97, 98, 104, 109,
    136
Dharma, 75
Diet, 113
Discipline, 42
Disinfectants, 117
Doctor, 112
Drink, 70
Duty, 157
Dvaita Dvaitism, 9

EARTHQUAKE, 22
Education, religious, 150
Ends and means, 35
Eternity, 21
Ethics, 115, 150
Europe, 36, 142
Evil, 6, 8, 22, 23, 52, 106,
    140
Evolution, 149

FABRI, Dr., 44-45
Faith, 2, 6, 10, 31, 33, 47,
    53, 54, 68, 85, 90-92,
    101, 104, 111, 126
Fast, 49-53
Fearlessness, 7
Flesh, bondage of, 117;
    mortification of, 51

Freedom, 24

GANDHISM, 4
Ganga, 65
Gayatri, 49
Generation, 127, 129
Gita, 19, 24, 47, 78, 79,
    92, 94, 95-104, 109,
    121, 132, 133, 135-137
God, 3-34, 42-43, 46, 59,
    62-64, 75-77, 79, 80, 82,
    83, 89-92, 96, 108, 109,
    110, 111, 115, 116, 118,
    119, 124, 126, 131-133,
    142, 144, 146, 147, 149,
    152
God, existence of, 5-10,
    11, 12, 13, 32, 81
God, law of, 4-8, 21-23,
    76, 83, 109, 148-150
God, names of, 10-13, 18,
    24, 42, 46, 62, 83, 84,
    108-110, 111
God, oneness of, 7-11, 19,
    60, 108-109
God is love, 6, 13, 15-17
God is Truth, 2, 7, 11, 12,
    18
God of gods, 80
God-realization, 30-34
Greece, 106
Guru, 74

HANUMAN, 46

Happiness, 131
Harishchandra, 20
Heathens, 65
Heber, Bishop, 65
Himalayas, 7, 10, 32
Himsa, 38, 102, 117
Hinduism, 53, 60-62, 69,
    72-75, 79, 80, 96, 97,
    139, 144
History, 149
Holy Ghost, 86, 87
Hospitals, 112
Humanitarianism, 73
Humility, 42, 86, 132, 139

IDEAL, RELIGIOUS, 150
Idol, idolatry, idol-
    worship, 74, 75, 80, 81,
    84, 86, 88, 90
Image, image-worship, 84-
    89
Imam Hasan & Imam
    Hussain, 20
Immortality, 111, 146
Incarnation, 82, 83, 91,
    94, 96
Inner Voice, see Voice of
    God
Insurance, 146
Ishwara, 10, 62, 81, 111
Islam, 11, 13, 53, 62, 69,
    72, 76, 79, 80, 144

JAIN, JAINISM, 10, 73

Janak, 3, 100
Janmashtami, 50
Japa, 49
Japan, 141
Jehova, 10
Jesus Christ, 37, 60, 67, 69, 77, 78, 82, 87, 106, 132, 142, 143, 144
Jonah, 52
Judaism, 69

KABIR, 132
Kalma, 13
Karmayogi, 135
Khuda, 10, 109, 111
Kingdom of Heaven, 3, 56, 147
Knowledge, 18, 97, 98, 100, 104
Koran, 60, 61, 74, 78, 107
Krishna, 42, 46, 77, 83, 84, 93, 94, 96, 104

LIFE, LAW OF, 15
Life, sacredness of, 73
Life, unity of, 4, 38, 73, 115-118
Lila, 8
Literalist, 93
Love, divine, 13, 15-17, 21
Love, law of, 16, 63, 130

MAHABHARATA, 93, 94, 96

Mammon, 142, 143
Mantras, 126
Marriage, 127-128
Mathews, Basil, 92
Maya, 8
Means and ends, 35, 146-147
Meat-eating, 69, 70
Miracles, 82
Missionaries, 65, 67, 70, 71
Moksha, 3, 118, 126
Moses, 60
Mosque, 61, 81, 82, 84-87
Mother, of Gandhiji, 87
Muhammed, 60, 61, 77, 82, 107, 132, 143
Muller, Max, 142
Music, 107

NAMAZ, 49
Nanak, 132
Narasimha Mehta, 47
Nature, 15, 20, 21, 25, 104, 105, 109, 110, 129
Nature Cure, 110-114
Nature's laws, 21, 22, 148
Newman, 7, 33
New Testament, 70, 79
Nineveh, 52
Nirvana, 77
Niyamas, 95
Non-possession, 14, 130-133

Non-violence, 4, 14, 16, 35, 36, 37, 73, 118, 141, 144

OMKAR, 109

PARAMATMA, 10
Pariahs, 66
Peace, of the soul, 99
Peace on Earth, 142-145
Phidias, 106
Politics, 3, 147-148
Poverty, 14, 133
Prahlad, 20
Prayer, 39-49, 53-55, 56, 89, 91, 112, 123, 135
Predestination, 148-149
Progress, 149
Prophet, 75, 91, 92
Proselytising, proselytism, 68, 69, 72
Puranas, 74
Purification, of self, 22, 40, 42, 50, 55, 56
Purity, 75, 107, 112

QUEST OF TRUTH, 1, 31, 59

RAHAMAN, RAHIM, 42, 46
Ram, Ramachandra, 10, 20, 33, 42, 46, 77, 83, 84, 93, 108-110

Ramabana, 111
Ramadas, 91
Ramakrishna, 132
Ramanama, 40, 108, 111, 112, 123, 126
Ramanuja, 10
Ramayana, 53, 93
Rationalism, rationalist, 90
Ravana, 23
Realization, 6, 31, 119
Reason, limitations of, 10, 31, 39, 74, 90, 92,, 93, 99, 108
Rebirth, 75, 149
Religion, 39, 53, 59-62, 68, 69, 75, 78, 101, 117, 150-151
Religion and politics, 3, 147
Religions, equality of, 59-62
Renunciation, 97, 98-103, 124, 131, 132, 144
Revelation, 32, 92
Revolution, 149
Rights, 151
Roman Catholics, 81, 82

SACRIFICE, 103, 104, 133, 135
Saint John, 67, 92
Saint Mathew, 92
Saint Theresa, 58

Saints, 81, 152
Salisbury, Lord, 67
Salvation, 3, 75, 84, 99-101, 106, 114
Sanatani, 73,
Sannyasa, 103
Sarvodaya, 137-140
Sat, 13, 18
Satan, 23, 50, 53, 142
Sat-Chit-Ananda, 18
Satvika, 132
Satya, 18, 19, 74
Satyagraha, 51
Satyavan, 88
Savitri, 88
Scripture, 74, 87, 92-95
Secrecy, 152
Self-control, 122, 128
Self-realization, 69, 97, 99, 105, 119
Self-surrender, 55
Sermon on the Mount, 77, 78, 106, 142
Service, of humanity, 3, 32, 47, 55, 71, 120, 131, 135, 136, 139
Sex-life, sex urge, 129
Shankara, 132
Shankaracharyas, 74
Shastras, 95
Shastris, 74
Shepperd, Dick, 17
Shiva, 10
Shuddhi, 72

Shudra, 93, 94
Silence, 57-59, 99
Sin, 22, 48, 84, 98, 129, 152-153
Sita, 84
Snake, 115, 118
Socrates, 106
Soul, 105, 106, 110-113
Soul-force, 35
Spinning, spinning wheel, 47, 48, 135
Spiritual force, 114
Spiritualism, 153-154
Sthitaprajnya, 109
Stopes, Marie, 129
Superstition, 84, 86-88, 91, 108, 154
Suradas, 40
Switzerland, 11
Syadvad, Syadvadi, 9
Symbolism, 75-84
Synagogue, 87

TABLIGH, 72
Tapas, 20
Temples, 61, 84-87
Time, 21
Tolerance, toleration, 60, 63-65, 143
Tolstoy, 143
Transmigration, 73
Trapist, 57
Tree-worship, 88-90
Truth, 1, 2, 4, 6, 7, 11-14,

18-20, 23, 25, 30-32, 34-36, 39, 59, 63, 65, 66, 74, 93, 95, 97, 102, 104-107, 116, 118-120, 130, 142, 147

Truth is God, 2, 11-14, 18-20, 23, 25, 30, 32, 34, 63, 108

Tulsidas, 91, 93, 108, 109

UNTOUCHABLES, 47, 66
Upanishads, 74
Utilitarian, 138

VAIRAGYA, 19
Vaishnava, 47
Varnashrama, 74
Vedas, 10, 60, 74, 77, 93, 94, 98
Vegetables, 117
Violence, 118, 140, 141
Virgin, Mary, 81-82, 84
Vishnu, 10

Visitations of Nature, 22
Vivisection, 113
Voice of God : Inner Voice, 14, 26-29
Still Small Voice, 32, 57, 93
Vow, 14, 89
Vyasa, 96

WALLACE, 143
War, 16, 36, 38, 141
Work, as worship, 133-137
Worship, 48, 61, 75, 83, 84, 85, 86, 88, 135, 136

YAJNA, 137
Yamas, 95
Yamuna, 65

ZEND AVESTA, 74
Zoroaster, 60, 77
Zoroastrianism, 53, 69